MASSACRE ROCKS
AND CITY OF ROCKS

Snake Country Series

Volume I
The Boise Massacre On The Oregon Trail
Attack on the Ward Party in 1854 and Massacres of 1859
(Published 2004)

Volume II
The Utter Disaster On The Oregon Trail
The Utter and Van Ornum Massacres of 1860
(Published 1993)

Massacre Rocks

and

City of Rocks

1862 Attacks on Emigrant Trains

by

Donald H. Shannon

Volume III
Snake Country Series

Snake Country Publishing
Caldwell, Idaho
2008

Library of Congress Control Number: 2008903134

ISBN   978–0–9635828–3–6

Snake Country Publishing
16748 W. Linden
Caldwell, ID 83607-9270
208–459–9233
snakecountryp@msn.com

Printed in the United States of America

Sons of Idaho Massacre Rocks Monument Dedication–1927

Five women are fully visible, two are partly seen, and an eighth is in the deep shadow with two men.

Idaho State Historical Society: #492–B–1, Massacre Rocks.

Contents

Illustrations

Figures

Maps

Preface

This volume, with Vol. I, *The Boise Massacre on the Oregon Trail* and Vol. II, *The Utter Disaster on the Oregon Trail,* form the trilogy of the Snake Country Massacres series. *The Boise Massacre on the Oregon Trail* covers the background of the Indians of the Snake Country, the attack on the Ward party in 1854, Army expeditions, and massacres of 1859. *The Utter Disaster on the Oregon Trail* details the Utter and Van Ornum Massacres of 1860.

This book is written more in the form of a 'chronicle' for an Audience who are interested in a detailed, comprehensive and orderly presentation of events so as to draw their own conclusions or interpretations. The quotes within this volume are faithful to the original forms, including spelling and punctuation. As noted below, eight sources are mainly cited in the text by a letter in superscript, instead of being referenced with an Arabic numeral.

The major sources of information for *Massacre Rocks and City of Rocks* come from chronological sequenced accounts: Chapter XVI: "Across the Plains to Oregon," from the 1887 book by Sherlock Bristol[B], *The Pioneer Preacher*; Henry M. Judson[J], Diary of 1862; Jane A. Gould[G] Tourtillott, Her Journal; John C. Hileman[H], Letter to Mrs. Marion W. Brownson, 11 August 1862; James S. McClung[JM], diary, 1862; Evans S. McComas[EM], A Journal of Travel 1862; Hamilton Scott[HS] diary, "Trip Across Plains in 1862;" and his brother, Robert C. Scott[RS], "Robert C. Scott's Trip To Washington With Oxen in 1862," diary, 12 January 1863.

The continuing assistance and material provided by (now retired) Idaho State Historian Larry Jones has been an invaluable contribution to this and the previous two books. His extensive, authoritative knowledge of the Oregon Trail has been most helpful. I wish to thank him and the staff of the Idaho State Historical Society Library and Genealogical Library for their continued support, and interest over the past quarter-century.

My thanks for the professional assistance provided over the years by the library staffs of the Oregon Historical Society; Oregon State Library; Oregon State Archives; Washington State Historical Society; Washington State Library; Utah State Historical Society; Nevada Historical Society; Nevada State Library; Idaho State Law Library; University of Idaho, Special Collections and Archives; University of Washington Libraries, Special Collections, Manuscripts and Archives; National Archives in the Microfilm Reading Room, Old Army Records, Cartographic Center, and Central Reading Room; LDS Genealogical Library; Golden Room of the California State Library; Canyon County Historical Society; and Owyhee County Historical Society. Thanks to Janet and Eric Shannon for reviewing the manuscript and to Janet for aid in the final editing.

Special thanks also and acknowledgment to the Nebraska State Historical Society, Tom Mooney, for permission to quote from the Diary of Henry M. Judson; the *South Idaho Press* for the use of the Almo Massacre legend; and the Idaho State Historical Society for the use of photos.

Cover photo: *Idaho State Historical Society: #278–A, Massacre Rocks.*

Twin Sisters, City of Rocks

Snake Country Massacres

<u>1854</u>

19 August	Attack on the Perry train on Jeffrey Cutoff in Camas Prairie (Elmore County, Idaho).
20 August	**Ward Massacre** along Boise River (south of Middleton, Canyon County, Idaho).

<u>1859</u>

26 July	Small emigrant train attacked at Twin Springs on the Hudspeth Cutoff (Oneida County, Idaho).
27 July	**Shepherd Massacre** west of Twin Springs on the Hudspeth Cutoff (Oneida County, Idaho).
12–13 August	Dragoon force fight Shoshoni in Box Elder canyon (between Cache Valley and Brigham City, Utah).
20 August	Ambush of the Carpenter Train on Kinney's Cutoff (near juncture of Idaho, Wyoming, Utah borders).
31 August	**Miltimore Massacre** in the vicinity of the American Falls (Power County, Idaho).

<u>1860</u>

23 June	Attack on Army Wagon Road Party between Malheur and Owyhee rivers (Malheur County, Oregon).
c26 August	Sheep Train Attacked at Castle Butte (Owyhee County, Idaho).
7–9 September	Wagon Train Attacked within five miles of City of Rocks (Cassia County, Idaho).
9–10 September	**Utter Massacre** along Snake River, west of Castle Butte (Owyhee County, Idaho).

c23 September	Two Ex-Dragoons from Utter Train killed on headwaters of John Day River (Grant County, Oregon).
c16–18 October	**Van Ornum Massacre** at Farewell Bend (Huntington, Baker County, Oregon).
1861	
	Soda Springs—Wagon Box Grave.
8 August	Stock taken from Harriman Train at City of Rocks.
1862	
15 July	Horses stampeded, Soda Springs, Idaho.
8 August	California miners attacked east of Fort Hall.
8 August	Smith train attacked east of City of Rocks.
9 August	Iowa train attacked City of Rocks.
9 August	Five Denver miners killed east of Fort Hall.
9 August	Attack on the Iowa City "Salmon River Party" Train and then the Adams Train east of **Massacre Rocks** (Power County, Idaho).
10 August	Attack on the Indians by members from several wagon trains near Massacre Rocks (Power County, Idaho).
15 August	Attack on Wagon Trains near City of Rocks (Cassia County, Idaho).
20 August	Bristol-Kennedy train skirmishes with Indians on Rock Creek (Twin Falls County, Idaho).
12 September	Eastbound Californians attacked by Shoshoni in a running fight on Salt Lake City road along Raft River, east of City of Rocks.
1863	
29 January	**Bear River Massacre**: California Volunteers attack Shoshoni on Battle Creek (Franklin County, Idaho).

... there is a monstrous emigration towards the Pacific, more than a thousand teams now on the plains ... Salmon River is now all the rage.

Dr. Charles Lewis Anderson

Introduction

It was two decades after the first wagon trains traversed the Oregon Trail that a number of emigrant-gold seekers set out from the Mid-west for the new gold strikes in the Rocky Mountains, in the rugged, remote Salmon River Mountains. Most knew not how to even reach the mines of "Fabulous Florence" north of the Salmon or "The Warrens" to the south —none of them knew of a way to get there with wagons.

Almost 300,000 people had traveled through the South Pass in the Rockies and into the Snake Country. Most had passed on through to California. Many were Latter Day Saints, Mormons, settling in Utah Territory, mainly around Salt Lake. Almost 60,000 had crossed the arid Snake River Plain and the Blue Mountains to found the settlements of the new state of Oregon and Washington Territory. The settlers west of the Cascade Mountains of that Territory were increasingly concerned as they began to be outnumbered by a floating population of stampeding miners hundreds of miles to the east.

As the bloody Civil War unfolded and some people in New England, New York City, and Oregon talked of secession from the Union, white men went throughout the land of the Shoshone saying that there was no more US government. The military presence in the west diminished with a depletion of defecting Southern officers, units being sent east to fight, and military posts being closed. The Shoshone Indians and the Bannock living among them, abetted by so-called "White Indians," became ever more brazen in their attacks on miners, freighters, and emigrant trains intruding into their land.

REV. SHERLOCK BRISTOL.

As pictured in his 1887 book, *The Pioneer Preacher*.

ONE

Changing Indian-White Relations

There was a great transformation in Indian-White relations in the Snake River Country in the historic twenty years of travel over the Oregon Trail. Medorem Crawford noted this change in 1862 when he led a military escort to the Pacific Northwest. Captain Crawford had escorted wagon trains over the emigrant road the year before. But that was not the first time he had been to Oregon. At age twenty-three, in 1842, he had traveled to the Willamette Valley when a few families first took wagons to the Columbia. He journeyed with, and encountered, legendary pioneers of this historic year of travel over the Oregon Trail, a year before large wagon trains began crossing.[1]

Crawford took a steamboat from St. Louis to Independence, Missouri and on 16 May 1842 left with the Lansford Hastings Train. On the trail this train of 17 wagons and 108 persons, including children, joined the wagons led by Dr. Elijah White. One of the Guides to pilot the trains was James Coates.

At the Green River crossing the party broke up. Some made pack saddles to use from there on, others were determined to take their wagons through and destroyed some to repair others. On 3 August Captain Hastings took the best wagons, left two that were not destroyed, and continued on with Stephen Meek as the Pilot.

Crawford's group of 27 men finished making pack saddles and started the next day with Tom Fitzpatrick as Captain and Pilot.

After an early start, on Wednesday 10 August, the emigrants saw fresh signs of Indians who soon came to them. These "Ponarchs" were Bannock or Shoshone and moving in the same direction. Many of these Indians traveled along with the party. When they struck the Bear river and camped, the entire group of Indians soon came up and camped nearby. Several horses were procured from the Indians, on reasonable terms. There was some more trading the next morning. The "soda springs and Boiling springs," were reached that day. There, some Indians came to the emigrant camp.

They continued on to the Snake River Plain, a geologic feature stretching about 400 miles across Southern Idaho, extending a little into Eastern Oregon. It is a wide flat bow-shaped arid agriculturally isolated area surrounded by mountains. The Plain was a natural avenue for wagon trains to use in traveling to Oregon.

When near Fort Hall Crawford's party camped by the Snake River and visited at the Hudson Bay Company trading post in the fort. While there, Hastings came into camp with the seven wagons he was captain of. On the 20th they saw American Falls and met a large number of Indians. Dr. White went back on the trail and traded with those Indians for fish and a horse.

The emigrants reached Goose Creek just after Hudson Bay Company packers, led by a Mr. McDonald, had arrived. Most of the emigrants, the Hastings party with wagons decided not to try to keep up with McDonald's party as their cattle were fatigued from the trip. But Dr. White's party left Goose Creek with the Hudson Bay Company packers on 23 August, intending to travel with them to Fort Vancouver. Crawford's company of packers were then left with only eight members, and no pilot.

As Crawford's party continued following along the south side of the Snake River, they "saw many Indians who live along the river and subsist principally on fish." Several times they passed

Indian lodges and a couple of camps containing many lodges. Some Indians would come to the emigrant camp for a meal. Several times the emigrants traded for both fresh and dry fish. They followed the South Alternate route of the Trail and on 31 August "rose a long hill" at Sinker Creek. After descending to the river they "found Indians pleanty towards evening. Camped near their village ... Many Indians come to camp traded pleanty of fish."

The emigrants left the land of the Shoshone and entered that of the Northern Paiute when they rejoined the main trail opposite the Hudson Bay Company's Fort Boise. On 3 September Crawford crossed over the Snake River in a canoe to the trading post. Crawford observed that Fort Boise "is a new Establishment. It has been a short time in operation but is not yet completed. We saw but one white man who was French." This was undoubtedly Francis Payette.

Crawford reached the Columbia by way of the Whitman Mission. On 14 September 1842 he noted that

> Our Indian Guide told us we would get to Dr. Whitman's today ...
>
> Dr. Whitman is a Missionary of the Presbyterian Order he has been in the Country six years. He has a verry comfortable house and is farming to a considerable extent. He has a Thrashing Machine & a grinding mill all under one roof driven by water power. Many Indians around him. I was never more pleased to see a house or white people in my life.[2]

After passing through the Columbia Gorge, Medorem Crawford reached "Willamut Falls" on 3 October. The distance from Independence to Willamette Falls according to his estimate was 1,746 miles. Some 125 people reached the Willamette valley using the Oregon Trail in 1842. Crawford recorded no adverse encounters with the Indians of the Snake Country.[3]

An early Oregon pioneer, Crawford was a provisional government legislator, 1847-1849, and a state legislator in 1860. He farmed near Dayton.

]   Army Escorts   [

The attack on the Carpenter Train, the attacks and Shepherd Massacre on the Hudspeth Cutoff, and the Miltimore Massacre at American Falls, all in 1859, led the Army to implement a strategy for protecting the emigrants on the Oregon Trail in the Snake Country. In 1860 the Department of Utah, from Camp Floyd, sent an expedition to the Portneuf River crossing, near the abandoned HBC Fort Hall. Troops were sent east toward South Pass to intercept and escort wagon trains. Escorts were provided west as far as Salmon Falls and south along the Raft River through City of Rocks.[*]

The Department of Oregon, sent an expedition from Fort Walla Walla to encamp on the Bruneau River on the South Alternate route of the Oregon Trail in Washington Territory. Patrols were sent east toward Salmon Falls to intercept the oncoming wagon trains. Escorts were provided on through to Oregon on the South Alternate and the main Trail through the Boise Valley. This worked well—the expedition returned to Fort Walla Walla after being told by the last trains passing through that there were no more trains behind. But, there was another train, one of eight wagons that had been traveling with a larger train headed for California. The unusual two-day attack on and taking of the Utter Train on the South Alternate and the subsequent attacks on the fleeing emigrants resulting in the Van Ornum Massacre, starvation, and captive children made this the greatest disaster to befall a wagon train in the Snake Country.[†]

---

*See Vol I, *The Boise Massacre on the Oregon Trail,* Chapter 18.
†See Vol II, *The Utter Disaster on the Oregon Trail.*

While this was occurring, Elias D. Pierce was discovering gold east of the Clearwater on Oro Fino Creek in the Nez Perce Indian Reservation in the northeast part of Washington Territory (now Idaho). In the subsequent rush for gold in the following months the strikes led toward the south and the mining camps of Pierce, Elk City, and, in the rugged Salmon River Mountains, "Fabulous Florence" were founded. The steamboat, "Idaho," was the main transporter of miners on the Upper Columbia to Lewiston, the newly established supply point where the Clearwater entered the Snake.

These gold strikes of 1861 by the "Idaho" miners were called the Salmon River mines and the Idaho mines. Shoshone County, established for the miners, soon had the largest population in Washington Territory. Those strikes over the Bitterroot Range of the continental divide were called the Upper Missouri mines.

Most of the US Army was stationed out West. As the Civil War unfolded many officers resigned their commissions to serve their states that seceded from the Union. Army garrisons were decimated with the defection of southerners and the withdrawal of regular soldiers for the battlefields of the east. Some posts were closed, among them the huge army base of Camp Floyd on Utah Lake. Most of the soldiers fighting in the Civil War, North and South, were in regiments raised and equipped by states rather than the federal government. In the Far West, volunteer units from Oregon and California were raised to take over the Army's duties. These citizen soldiers had little reservation about killing Indians. The native population of Northern California had been pretty much exterminated in the previous decade. In the aftermath of the Ward Massacre in the Boise Valley in 1854 and the resulting army expeditions of that year and the next, a general Indian war occurred throughout the Pacific Northwest, not ending until 1858.

In 1861 emigrant travel over the Oregon Trail was light compared to previous years. In July, a party of seven men, came

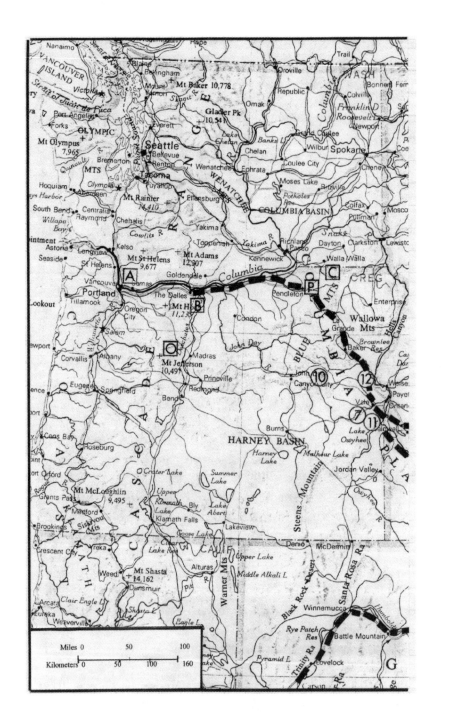

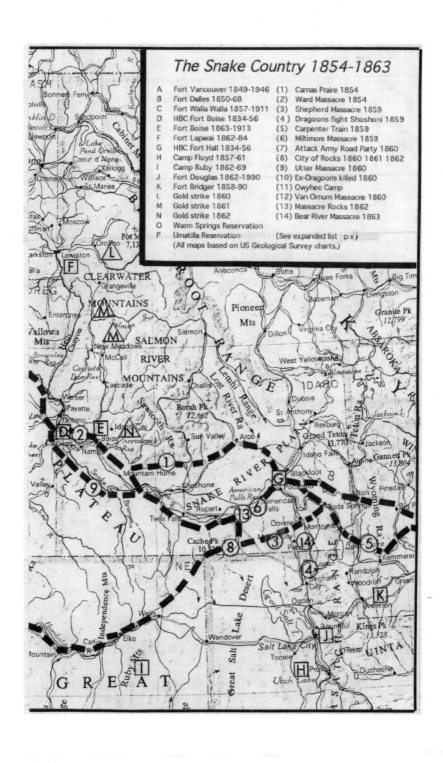

The Snake Country 1854-1863

A	Fort Vancouver 1849-1946	(1)	Camas Praire 1854
B	Fort Dalles 1850-68	(2)	Ward Massacre 1854
C	Fort Walla Walla 1857-1911	(3)	Shepherd Massacre 1859
D	HBC Fort Boise 1834-56	(4)	Dragoons fight Shoshoni 1859
E	Fort Boise 1863-1913	(5)	Carpenter Train 1859
F	Fort Lapwai 1862-84	(6)	Miltimore Massacre 1859
G	HBC Fort Hall 1834-56	(7)	Attack Army Road Party 1860
H	Camp Floyd 1857-61	(8)	City of Rocks 1860 1861 1862
I	Camp Ruby 1862-69	(9)	Utter Massacre 1860
J	Fort Douglas 1862-1990	(10)	Ex-Dragoons killed 1860
K	Fort Bridger 1858-90	(11)	Owyhee Camp
L	Gold strike 1860	(12)	Van Ornum Massacre 1860
M	Gold strike 1861	(13)	Massacre Rocks 1862
N	Gold strike 1862	(14)	Bear River Massacre 1863
O	Warm Springs Reservation		
P	Umatilla Reservation	(See expanded list p x)

(All maps based on US Geological Survey charts.)

over the Blue Mountains and onto the Snake River Plain to meet relatives coming west on the Oregon Trail. They had pack animals carrying food and supplies that they expected the arriving emigrants would need. A.B. Roberts had seven packs of provisions and five or six saddle horses. He cached some packs at the Malheur River crossing (Vale, Oregon). In the afternoon one of the men, Henry Watson, and Roberts went on Malheur Butte, "the great butte across the river where we could see for many miles around. We could see a great camp of nearly 1,000 Indian wigwams down towards Snake river but no emigrants on the road to the East."[4]

Roberts traveled along the South Alternate as far a the Three Island Crossing but saw no emigrants on the trail. They stopped and examined the scene of the Utter Massacre. Not knowing whether the wagon trains were taking the Camas Prairie route or where they were, the party of seven started their return to Walla Walla. "No incident of importance occurred on our return until we reached the Owyhee … Here we met a "big scare" again. Below us and near the Snake and Owyhee were what looked to be 1000 Indian wigwams. The Watsons refused to go into camp … At near sundown the Watsons and Dennys pulled out for the Malheur."

On returning to the Malheur crossing they found that Roberts' cache of three pack loads of provisions had been dug up and was gone. Later he learned that the Watsons

> had met E.D. Pierce with a party of prospectors who was getting short and told him that they had a cache which they could not need and that he was welcome to the supplies.
>
> So we pushed on and saw no human being until we reached the Umatilla where we found Zeph Bryant, an

*See Vol II, *The Utter Disaster on the Oregon Trail*, Appendix III.

acquaintance of mine from the lower Columbia and his party of prospectors.[5]

After "nearly two months of a strenuous journey" Roberts returned to Walla Walla. His brother-in-law, Captain Hawley, with three packs and Mr. Bryant, again, left to meet the emigrants. When

> they began the descent into the Burnt river canyon the first weary wagon train was met. This train reported almost continuous conflict with Indians after crossing the Rockies and all the way down the Snake river and assured Capt. Hawley that it was unsafe and useless to go on, as the body of the emigration was behind and under a government escort. But Mr. Hawley had grit and was fully determined to push on and meet his family as soon as possible. So they pushed on down the great canyon and over to the horrible Snake country and across the deserts to the Malheur meeting emigrants frequently all of whom assured them that their efforts were hazardous and useless.[6]

They met Samuel King's train which had a serious fight with Indians at the Owyhee. Hawley and Bryant returned with the King Train to Burnt river where they decided to wait. After only one day the Indians became so numerous that the two went further west, back into the Grande Ronde valley. They found some emigrants were actually building homes there. The relatives and

> friends were with the escort and had been for several hundred miles, as Capt. Madorum Crawford of the escort had borrowed their light rig to send forward assistance and broken it, after which they were given a government wagon and were taken into the government train for the

balance of the journey. It was said that after my letter written on the tin was found far up on Snake river and being thus evidence that friends were out making an effort to assist them, Capt. Crawford was very solictious with his assistance. So possibly my efforts were of some account after all.

This "government escort" was taken up on account of the various massacres during the previous years and was continued for three seasons. It was not composed of U.S. soldiers, but was only in command of an army officer. It was made up by enlisting 100 young men who wanted to go to the Far West and who were willing to be discharged at the end of the trip. Many of these young men became useful and prominent citizens of the Walla Walla Valley while others went to adjacent mines and some to Oregon. Two of these escorts were disbanded at Fort Walla Walla and the third at Fort Boise, it being the policy of the government to disband the escort upon reaching the first military post.[7]

Some Members of Wagon Trains–1862

Iowa City "Salmon River Party." Mule train of 11 wagons.

Capt. Andrew J. Hunter	Iowa City, Johnson Co, IA
A.J. Cassady, Teacher, age 30	Iowa City, Johnson Co, IA
Hiram Watts, age 53	Iowa City, Johnson Co, IA
(& family?)	
Edmund Harrison, Printer, age 30	Iowa City, Johnson Co, IA
(& family?)	
Charles M. Harrison* (Hainson)	Iowa City, Johnson Co, IA
John C. Henley, lawyer, age 26	Iowa City, Johnson Co, IA
Joseph E. Fales, clerk, age 58	Iowa City, Johnson Co, IA
Isaac Ijams	Iowa City, Johnson Co, IA
John Wilson, age 43, was Sheriff of	Johnson Co, IA
(& family?)	
Jas. P. Olcot, Merchant, age 30	Iowa City, Johnson Co, IA
Henry Murray, Physcian, age 47	Iowa City, Johnson Co, IA
(& family?)	
Masemo Lepi (Massimo Lippi)	an Italian, St. Paul, MN
Giovanni Benvenuti	an Italian, St. Paul, MN
Following in one wagon:	
Pangburn	Leavenworth, KS
Bernard	Leavenworth, KS
Coreys	Leavenworth, KS
[Mrs. Ellen Jones (?) & husband]	

Adams Train. Ox train of 13 wagons.

George W. Adams	Madison, IA
Mrs. Adams	Madison, IA
dau. Elizabeth 'Lizzie' Adams, age 26	Madison, IA
son Thomas J. Adams	Madison, IA
son George W. Adams, age 24	Madison, IA
Charles Bulwinkle (Bullwinkel)	New York City, NY
George Leeper (Sheperd, Sheperi, Liffe)	Iowa City, IA
William Leeper (brother to George)	Iowa City, IA
[Mrs. Ellen Jones (?) & husband]	

---

*Those who kept journals or later wrote accounts of their journey are indicated in bold print.

Some Members of Wagon Trains–1862. (Compiled by Author.)

Kennedy Train. (Newman, "Newbern Colony.")

Ox train 62 (40 or 36) wagons from Iowa.

Kennedy family, from Mahaska Co, IA, settled in Union county, Oregon:

Capt. John Knox Kennedy	51
Mrs. Sarah McGuire Stoot Kennedy	46
? Kennedy (a married sister)	
Mary E. Kennedy (m. Allison)	20
John U.C. Kennedy	12
Margaret A. Stoot (m. Ewing, Thiel)	16 b. 18 Mar 1846
Susan Jane Stoot (m. Neeley)	
Cassie Stoot (m. Caviness)	
(brother) Stoot	

(Nine in the family besides the hired man)

McGuire, John

Mary Jane McGuire

Taylor Family, from near Oskaloosa, IA, settled at Walla Walla W. T:

Mr. Ephraim Taylor	37
Mrs. Nancy Taylor	31
Martha Jane Taylor 14 (from Ephraim's previous marriage?)	
Ezra, Taylor	13
John Wesley Taylor	11
James Madison Taylor	9
William Burton Taylor	7
Christena "Teen" **Taylor** (m. Howard) b. 17 Apr 1857 Mahaska, IA	
Ephraim Taylor, Jr.	3
Albert Taylor (2 men with Taylors):	
Hatcher	
Henly	

D. Y. Collins		
Hamilton Scott	IA	
Robert C. Scott	IA	
Wilson Scott	IA	
Lewis Beck	IA	
Lem Jones	IA	
Rev. Joseph Paul and family	55	Mahaska Co, IA
Mrs. Mary Paul	51	
Mercy Paul, youngest daughter		
son, Thomas Paul and family	41	Fremont IA
Mrs. Elizabeth Paul	aged 32 years	
Louisa J. Paul (m. Estes)	12	

Some Members of Wagon Trains–1862 (cont.).

Mary Melvina Paul	10
Isaac E. Paul	9
Harriett E. Paul	7
Patsy Alice Paul	5
Lucinda Arletta Paul	2
Paul infant	

Zaring family, from Oskaloosa, IA, settled at Walla Walla W. T.

Mr. **Alvin Zaring**	b. 2 December 1837, Indianapolis IN
Mrs. Mercy Paul Zaring	22
Ezra Eli I. Zaring	3 years old

(Another Zaring child, Roy?, also made the journey)

Sarah Alice Zaring [m. Howard]

Mary Rayburn, young German who took care of Thomas Paul children

Thomas Newman	Oskaloosa, Mahaska Co, IA
John Tool	
William DeLong	
Mr. Townsend	Monroe, IA
Mrs. Townsend	Monroe, IA
Wife of Tim Bailey	
Bailey infant	
George Bove (accident shot self 4 July 1862)	Batavia, Wapello Co, IA
Mrs. Bovee (Bove) and two children	Jefferson Co, IA
Thomas Mackay	
E.E. Ellis	
wife and infant	
A. Hunter	
Mrs. Hoover	
James S. McClung	Wappello, IA
William Redhoffer	

Party from Pikes Peak mines.
(About three wagons.)

Young, tried and executed for murder of Scott.
Scott, shot and killed by Young.

Some Members of Wagon Trains–1862 (cont.).

<u>Bristol Train</u>. 79 mule or horse-drawn wagons. (Judson list.)

Capt Rev. **Sherlock Bristol**	Dartford, Green Lake Co, WI
Rev. J.W. Walcott	Ripon, Fon Du Lac Co, WI
G. Bainan (Beynon)	Ripon, Fon Du Lac Co, WI
William McKinnon (McKimson)	Ripon, Fon Du Lac Co, WI
W.G. Ives	Fulton City, IL
Joshua Hollingshead	Fulton City, IL
Thomas Fletcher	Rosendale, WI
L.W. Coe	Ripon, Fon Du Lac Co, WI
Charles Combs	Ripon, Fon Du Lac Co, WI
Jason D. Smith	Rosendale, WI
Nathan Hunter	Ripon, Fon Du Lac Co, WI
A.B. Thrall	Ripon, Fon Du Lac Co, WI
J.H. Eugh	Ripon, Fon Du Lac Co, WI
Alexander R. Hargrave	Ripon, Fon Du Lac Co, WI
E.M. Geiger & wife	Quincy, IL
& wife	Quincy, IL
C.W. Geiger, 4 yrs. old	Quincy, IL
Robert McComb	Lewiston, IL
James Phillips	Fairplay, Grant Co, WI
Robert Phillips	Fairplay, Grant Co, WI
Daniel Hunsaker	Fairplay, Grant Co, WI
Eugene Smith	Fairplay, Grant Co, WI
7. John Lockwood*	Steamboat, Rock Co, IA
8. Engle	
9. Hurst	
William H. Shepard	Mankato, Blue Earth Co, MN
W. Kegerreis	Mankato, Blue Earth Co, MN
Ferdinand C. Roosevelt	Mankato, Blue Earth Co, MN
H. R. Meeker & wife	LaCrosse, LaCrosse Co, WI
Frank A. Ford	Sparta, Monroe Co, WI
4. Joseph W. Sprott "Joe"	Chariton, Lucas Co, IA
5. William Henry Humphrey, age 31	Chariton, Lucas Co, IA
("Hank", the "Jack Screw")	
6. Henry "Hank" C. Byerly (Ryerly), 18	Chariton, Lucas Co, IA
2. **John C. Hileman**	Omaha, Douglas Co, NE
1. **Henry M. Judson** "Judd"	Omaha, Douglas Co, NE

---

*The 13 numbered individuals were part of, or joined, the Omaha & Salmon River Mining and Equip. Co. prior to joining the Bristol Train on 4 July 1862.

Some Members of Wagon Trains–1862 (cont.).

3. Redfield "Red"	
11. J. P. Manning "Joe"	Omaha, Douglas Co, NE
12. John Mellus (Mellers Mellas)	Omaha, Douglas Co, NE
10. Mr. Russel	
13. Thomas H Parkes	Elkhorn, Douglas Co, NE
Charles Freeman wife & child (babe)	MN
wife & child (babe)	MN
E.A. Temple & wife	Ottumwa, Wapello Co, IA
Caroline	Ottumwa, Wapello Co, IA
William Michaels	Ottumwa, Wapello Co, IA
William Chandler	Ottumwa, Wapello Co, IA
Miss Chandler	
S.M. Rice	NY
W.P. Roberts	Belmont, LaFayette Co, WI
14. John H. Jones	Pickatonie, Iowa Co, IA
15. Dr. Henry Owens	Pickatonie, Iowa Co, IA
Dr. William B. Jones	Belmont, LaFayette Co, WI
wife & two boys	
Edward Wait	Beaver Dam, Dodge Co, WI
Peter B. Laraway	Beaver Dam, Dodge Co, WI
James Durant	Calamus , Dodge Co, WI
Fred K. Henry Martin	Buffalo, Erie Co, NY
Edward Sapp	Farmington, Fulton Co, IL
William Scott	Apple River Station, WI
J.K. Root	Cedar Rapids, Linn Co, IA
Sam Clemens	Cedar Rapids, Linn Co, IA
Mrs. Bailey	Cedar Rapids, Linn Co, IA
Merit P. Gibson	Comanche, IA
Luther Dickey	Iowa City, Johnson Co, IA
C.W. (M) Westfall (William, age 17)	Iowa City, Johnson Co, IA
together:	
2 Germans one with a wife from	Denver
Mr. Wheeler (City Express wagon)	
Jake Sheppard	French
Jeager	

Walker Ox Train. (Wilson Train joined making 73 (?) wagons.)

Capt. John P. Walker
Juliette G. Walker
little child run over by a wagon
Mr. Thomas Bradford (blacksmith)

Some Members of Wagon Trains–1862 (cont.).

Wilson Train

Capt. Wilson
    Mrs. Wilson
    Wilson baby
Gould family from Mitchell Co, IA, settled at Stockton, CA
    Mr. Albert H. Gould   died 1863
    Mrs. **Jane Augusta Holbrook Gould [Tourtillott]**, b 1833–d 1917
    George Albert Gould (son)   born 1853–died 1921
    Frank Horace Gould (son)   born 1855
    Mr. Gould (Albert's father)?
    Lucy "Lou" Gould Wyman (Albert's sister)
    Charles A. Wyman (Lou's husband)
    Gus
Annie McMillin
Mr. Bullwinkle, left 25 July, joined Adams train
German physician
Mr. Church
Mr. Neff

Jack and Carseley Train. Denver company.

Captain William Jack
Captain William Carseley
E. S. McComas   age 23
C.(Corneil?) M. Westfall
George Walker
Luther Dickey
Don Clark
Bill McFate
Sam Hindman
Neil Howie (Howey)   Madison, Wisc.
Dave Rook
Mrs. Mann
Tom Laven
Baldwin
Watson

Some Members of Wagon Trains–1862 (cont.).

TWO

Immigration of 1862

While along the Snake River with the 1st Oregon Cavalry, Colonel Rueben F. Maury estimated that in 1862 some 8,000 persons in 1,300 wagons passed to the Northwest.[EM] This was in marked contrast to the seven preceding years when the immigration there ranged from 500–2,000.[1]

Things were changing along the Oregon Trail. The Pony Express was in operation, stagecoach service was provided to California, and telegraph lines had reached South Pass. In the Northwest, James Warren was leading a prospecting party which crossed the Salmon River canyon to the south of the mines around Florence—and discovered gold in The Warrens. Other prospectors were striking out and would discover gold in the Boise Basin. Others, in the Deer Lodge Valley and the Upper Missouri of what would become Montana.

George Chandler "had no thought of going to Oregon. He was headed for California, but ... the discovery of wonderful gold deposits in the Salmon River district in Idaho some thirty miles from Lewiston" changed his mind. "We heard of the unprecedented richness of these mines and decided to go there"[2]

The Secretary of War assigned Captain Medorem Crawford, the duty of leading an expedition from Omaha, Nebraska Territory to Portland, Oregon. The expedition was to provide an escort for the protection of travelers along the emigrant road to Oregon. Crawford organized a cavalry company of fifty mounted men who were armed with rifles and revolvers. After taking an oath of allegiance at Camp Stanton, four miles from Omaha, the civilians were "enrolled into the service of the government of the United States." They were instructed in the duties of sentinels and were drilled in the simpler evolutions of cavalry tactics.[3]

Leroy Crawford, of New York, and James M. Pyle, of Oregon, were the Lieutenants. George D. Thomas, of Illinois, and J.B. Ames, of New York, were appointed assistants (to aid Crawford); Dr. J.A. Chapman, of New York, surgeon; Samuel Gillespie Crawford, of New York, clerk; and Austin Badger, of New York, wagon-master. Samuel Crawford was Medorem's father and Leroy was his brother. The company was divided into three squads, each with a sergeant and corporal. "So complete was this system of organization, and so vigilant were the officers and men, that no animals strayed or were stolen between Omaha and Walla-Walla."[4]

On 16 June the Escort left Omaha and followed along the north side of the Platte River. On the 28th, opposite Fort Kearney, the first emigrants joined the Escort. At South Pass they took the Lander Road and passed near Fort Hall. They then rejoined the older route of the Oregon Trail, crossing the Snake River Plain along the south side of Snake River. At the Bruneau River crossing on the South Alternate they met the encamped First Oregon Cavalry. The Escort again joined the main route of the Trail just inside Oregon and crossed over the Blue Mountains to Fort Walla Walla. On 30 October, over four months after starting, Crawford made his report of the principal incidents of the trip.

> The movement westward was very large. Emigrants to Oregon, Washington Territory, California, Salt Lake, and Denver were on this road. Some had started in April, and were consequently several hundred miles in advance of

the rear portion of the emigration. Feeling it to be my duty to protect the rear, I did not hasten on the first part of the trip, but urged upon the emigrants whom I fell in with as I proceeded the necessity of husbanding the strength of their teams so as to be able to perform the journey over the barren deserts of Snake River, the necessity for which my last year's experience had taught me.[5]

After twenty years, emigrant travel over the Oregon Trail was well established. Most wagon trains were fairly small with only ten to fifteen wagons and had a following of extra stock when they started their journey. There were a number of trains, often only a few miles apart.[6] The emigrants mostly used oxen to pull their wagon, but some used mules. Because of the different gaits of these two types of draft animals, rarely did you see a train employing both.

In this second year of the Civil War, most of the emigrants traveling the Oregon Trail along the Platte River Road were from Iowa. Almost all crossed the Missouri from Council Bluffs to Omaha. The daily journals kept by some half-dozen of these emigrants described the often-detailed events that transpired on their journey of travel. Other emigrants wrote letters describing the events. In later years some were interviewed about the happenings or wrote accounts of their adventures.

One group of emigrants came from the central part of Eastern Iowa. It was a mule train that started out from Iowa City as the "Salmon River Party." It was identified as the "Iowa City Train" by other emigrants on the trail (and for some reason later called the "Smart Train"). Andrew J. Hunter was the captain of this train of eleven wagons—the size of a train was generally reckoned in number of wagons.

Another emigrant from the same county, Johnson County, Iowa, but traveling in a different train, was Evan Smith McComas. He was born in Adams County, Ohio, on 23 January

1839. The 23-year-old McComas "was a southern sympathizer of Kentucky, Ohio, and Indiana antecedents. He was not interested in enlisting, nor in the possibility of being drafted to fight for Father Abraham. He was, in the phrase of the day, a species of Galvanized Yankee. He came West to avoid going South." He was not the only young man who headed West to distance himself from the fighting.[EM]

McComas kept a journal. "Started May 14th 1862 at 3 o'clock from home to 'Washington Territory.' Company: George Walker, C.M. Westfall, Luther Dickey, E.S. McComas." This party left Omaha on 2 June.[EM]

George W. Adams and his family were emigrating from Madison (or Marion) County, just south of Des Moines. He was captain of an ox train of thirteen wagons, known as the Adams Train.[7]

]   The Kennedy Train   [

James S. McClung left Wapello, Iowa on 22 April for "the gold diggins of Salmon River."[JM] Near Fremont, Iowa the Paul family formed a party for a trip by ox train to Walla Walla, Washington Territory. Rev. Joseph Paul and wife, Mary, were in the party. Also Joseph's son, Thomas Paul, his wife Elizabeth, and their six children with the eldest being Louisa. Also included was the Reverend's youngest daughter, Mercy Paul Zaring and husband, Alvin.[8] Three Scott brothers, Robert, Wilson, and Hamilton were in this party, along with Lewis Beck, Lem Jones, and other friends around Fremont. Joseph Paul was selected as captain. They loaded their wagons and started on 24 April, driving "eight miles. Our teams worked very well. We had three yoke of oxen and one yoke of cows to a team. Our first camp was three miles east of Oskaloosa."[HS] "As Captain Joseph Paul was a minister, each Sunday religious services were held."[RS]

Louisa J. Paul, then 12, noted "The first stop we made was at my Aunt and Uncle Parley's, my father's sister and husband, at Palmyra, Iowa, a small country town, where we stayed a week." They left "Mahaska County, for this Western Country May first 1862."[9]

Five-year-old Christina "Teen"Taylor recalled that "her parents, Ephraim and Nancy Taylor, started from Iowa in May, 1862. They had oxen and two covered wagons. There were eight children, and two men traveled with them." They were from near Oskaloosa—a neighbor, John Knox Kennedy, led the train.[10]

Kennedy had two daughters and a couple of sons. He was widowed, then married Sarah McQuire Stoot, who probably had a son and three daughters. Her daughter Margaret was also including step-siblings when she recalled, "My two brothers, my four sisters, two of whom were married, with myself and mother and stepfather, started from Iowa on May 5 ... There were nine in our family besides the hired man." (An older brother, Robert Kennedy, was around Walla Walla and the mines, having crossed in 1857.) Kennedy "bought four riding horses and four side-saddles" for Margaret and her sisters.[11]

My stepfather, John Kennedy, sold our place in Mahaska county, Iowa, and turned all of our property into money. Nine other families near us wanted to come West, so they promised that if my stepfather would buy wagons and oxen for them and outfit them to cross the plains they would return the money he spent, with good interest, when they got out to Oregon. He outfitted these nine families. When they got out there they promised him that if they ever got any money ahead that they could spare they would pay him what they owed, but he never got a cent from them.

We laid in enough provisions to last four months, for he figured that we could make the trip in that length of time ... They elected my stepfather captain as he had already made two round trips across the plains.[12]

The Paul and Kennedy parties departed Omaha around 20 May. James McClung also noted that John K. Kennedy was elected captain of the fifty-two wagon train while it was at Rawhide Creek.[JM] The census of the train was taken on the North Platte on 8 June. Hamilton and Robert Scott recorded, "There was 88 men, 69 women, 86 children under 18 years in the company, totaling 243 in all. The train consisted of 52 wagons, covered by canvas, drawn by oxen. There was 315 head of oxen, 38 head of saddle horses, 14 mules, 38 milk cows, a total of 405 head of stock in all."[RS]

From Northeastern Iowa came an emigrant party who would travel in a different train, heading for California. The Gould family departed from Chickasaw County on 27 April. There were some eight in the family with Mrs. Jane Augusta Holbrook Gould (born 1833) keeping a diary. On 14 May, "Some of the men stood guard over the teams, we having heard of some of the emigrants losing horses." The next day they crossed the "old Missouri" on the ferry boat "Lizzy Baylis." On 4 June, "Camped near the banks of the Platte again. Here the men partly organized, chose their captain, his name is Wilson, he has been through to California once before."[G]

]   The Bristol Train   [

Sherlock Bristol was a Congregational Clergyman[J] of Fon du Lac County, Wisconsin. He was born 15 June 1815, Cheshire, New Haven County, Connecticut. He would later, in 1887, publish a detailed book of his life. But, in early 1862 he[B]

suffered from sick headache about one-third of the time, and the average of sleep was not more than one night in three. I needed not only physical exercise but change

—something to get the mind out of the old ruts, the grooves it had worn so deep. Then came the happy thought of a trip across the plains, with covered wagon drawn by oxen or horses, and plodding along for six months, with little opportunity for reading books or mental exercise, and an abundance of calls for muscular employment. Very opportune for my plans was the discovery of the "Salmon River mines."[B]

Bristol formed a company with a number of his neighbors who were eager to go together over the plains. In March[B]

three four-horse wagons, covered with white canvas, filed through the streets of Ripon, each having a complement of four men, all well known and substantial citizens, and bound for the Pacific coast. A large crowd gathered around us to bid us good-bye and pour upon us showers of good wishes and hopes of success and a safe return. Some one of the crowd wrote in large letters on the wagon I was in, "Capt. Bristol's Train." I don't know who it was, but our good-natured company of twelve accepted the suggestion, and so called me Captain after that. My messmates were Deacon Bainan, McKinnon, and Principal Walcott, the latter long time the head of the Ripon Academy and embryo college.[B]

They traveled via Madison, Galena, and Des Moines to the Missouri River. At Council Bluffs they "laid in our supplies for a journey of two thousand miles, and which was to occupy the following six months and more." They crossed to Omaha and then drove along the north side the Platte River. As several other emigrant teams fell in with them they organized a company. Bristol "was unanimously chosen Captain. I did not relish the office, on account of its care and responsibility, for I wanted rest and freedom from care; but I accepted, chiefly because it would enable me to secure <u>the keeping of the Sabbath</u>."[B]

]   Judson and Hileman   [

Henry M. Judson arrived in Omaha, Nebraska in 1856 and became the proprietor of the Hamilton House.[13] In 1862 "Judd" Judson and John C. Hileman, both from Omaha, and a third partner, "Red" Redfield, called themselves the Omaha & Salmon River Mining & Equipment Company. On 5 June they made their "grand exit" from Omaha bound for the new gold regions. Their outfit consisted of five mules, a light wagon, "a good mooring tent," provisions, mining implements, clothing, etc.[J]

By the second day they naturally fell into their respective positions of responsibility: Hileman handling the stock; Redfield the tent, bedding, and miscellaneous; and Judd the culinary duties.[J]

On the fifth day they joined with a party of three men with an outfit similar to their own. They were from near Chariton, Iowa: Joseph W. Sprott, Henry "Hank" C. Ryerly, and William Henry Humphrey. The latter was a healthy, stout fellow whom Hileman dubbed "the Jack Screw" from the facility with which he lifted their wagon for greasing the wheels. (In his journal Judson referred to Ryerly as "Hank" and Humphrey as "Jack.") The next day, 10 June, Judson learned "by Mr. Hayes of the ferry that the second edition of the Omaha & Salmon river mining & Equip Co. left Omaha on the eve of Monday the 9th. We also learn of the raid of the Sioux among the Pawnees only ten miles from our camp & of the Killing of 14 of the Pawnee & one Sioux." [J]

Bristol had more information on this raid. While encamped on the Loup Fork one evening we

> heard a din of doleful voices, proceeding from the tepees, or tents of buffalo hides, occupied by a band of Pawnees near by. Our sympathies were excited, and a man and I went over to see what was the matter. Some of them could talk English, and they told us with artless

simplicity, how that some weeks before they heard that a band of adjacent Sioux Indians had gone on a buffalo hunt, leaving large numbers of ponies, their wives and children, in a defenceless condition. This was too good an opportunity to rob and to kill to be neglected; so a band of their young braves, like young eagles, made haste for the prey. Alas for Indian sagacity and rapacity in this case? The young Pawnees met the Sioux on the border, were defeated, some of them slain, and the remainder put to ignominious flight! Hence these tears, these ululations which had aroused our pity. My companion and I went back to our camp much less inclined to weep than when on our way to visit them. Years afterward—some eight or ten—when Miss "Bright Eyes," the Pawnee Indian girl, was moving Boston audiences by her tales of wrongs done by white people to long-suffering Pawnees and other Indian tribes, this scene came up very vividly before me.[B]

Opposite Fort Kearney on 15 June, the emigrants "bid adieu to civilization & enter upon camp duties & life in earnest - No more meet or pass the stage & habitations of civilized man. We now enter a new country & entirely new scenes - I sincerely hope that adventures to be recorded here may be scarce - We here form our guard or night watch the party consisting ... of four teams -10 men & 14 head of mules & horses."[J]

Sunday the 22nd they are overtaken and called upon by Manning, Mellus, and Parks. "They are in co with one of the McFaddens & his sister who drive on & leave them in our camp." The three men decided to go on with Judson's party. Five days later, "Redfield is taken suddenly ill & lies down by the road with his tobacco pouch & brandy bottle - He was got into the wagon & by eve camp recovered - I gave him in the mean time 2 blue pills - think he will be ok in the morning."[J]

The 28th Judson "Passed a half breed's lodge (Borries an acquaintance of Redfields) & a trading post also the lodge of a full blood Sioux - Met a Mormon freight of 40 wagons & probably 400 head of cattle" heading east to Florence, the Mormon wintering and staging area near Omaha. "Passed a train nearly as large bound for Salmon River"[J]

Two days after he fell "ill" Redfield was left near Rawhide Creek at a French Indian trader's place where he proposed to pass the day. "Red field came back just before supper sulky & sullen as ever." The next day, 30 June, "We are all astonished this morning by the refusal of Redfield to go along with the party or to permit the team to go - the cause he assigns is that some of the party have insulted him - The party has used all of us well only cracking jokes on each other & he does not appear willing to take what he gives."[J]

"Jack," Hank Humphrey "the Jack Screw," insisted on giving Redfield "a drubbing but restrains himself by a strong effort - Hileman tries persuasion - no use - makes one proposition after another - but no use - finally gets tired beyond his patience & begins to harness the wheel mules - Redfield sneaks up & takes the lariat off of one & starts him out on the prairie loose - then while I try to catch him he cuts the lariats from the rest & swears the train shall not go - Hileman mounts the mule he was harnessing & goes after the lot which take the direction of a Frenchman's ranch & herd." Soon Hank Humphrey, Joe Manning and some others go to Hilemans assistance while Judson finished packing their things. "Redfield goes down to the Lodge and there they have more high words & more propositions or rather a repetition of the old ones but to no effect - Red sees the probability of the boys getting the mules coming back in advance of the party says tis all settled - sneaks up & takes off the nuts from the wagon wheels on one side & starts down the river & hides or pretends to hide them."[J]

When everyone had arrived back in camp "the proposals of Hileman are renewed & he also loudly calls for proposals from Red but gets none but the old one to abandon the party ..." The three partners had so many times been assisted by the others, whom Hileman and Judson "can see no wrong but on the contrary have ever received the kindest & most gentlemanly treatment - Would we could report the same of Red." Hank Humphrey and Joe finally make some "leather knees" and put them on the wagon (to keep the wheels on). Judson loads[J]

> Reds baggage which he says should go with the rest of his property but he does not wish to aid the start by putting it on himself - I "mount the boys" & off we go leaving Red with his grey mule "Tom" - the saddle bridle - white coat - Knife & pistol & tobacco pouch - Once the wheel comes nearly off but we stopped in time to save it - its soon repaired & we finish the drive of 12 miles for dinner & camp near another Frenchman's lodge.[J]

Judson wondered what will become of the three partners' Omaha & Salmon River Mining & Equipment Company. The "operation remains to be seen though we now have the best" of Redfield and "to pay for such dastardly treatment we propose to keep it." In the afternoon as they started to drive on they saw "Redfield coming up in sight before we leave & stopping to talk with the Frenchman - We drive 8 miles to Rawhide Creek a dry stream bed & just as we camp Redfield rides by us - For safety we double our guard - load all our arms & pass a rather uncomfortable night but without disturbance."[J]

] Fort Laramie [

Daniel McLaughlin, en route for the Salmon River, reached Fort Laramie on 24 July. From the time he left Omaha, "we passed at least 20,000 persons in ox wagons, drays, carts and every describable species of rotary vehicles, and on foot, making diurnal and some nocturnal efforts to reach Salt Lake, Nevada, California, Oregon, and Salmon River." About Fort Laramie "the horse and mule teams got the start and commenced forming companies of the persons who were destined to the same points. We fell in and joined a crowd bound for Salmon River."[14]

When Sherlock Bristol arrived at Fort Laramie he "resigned my captaincy, and another was chosen; but after two days of service my successor resigned and I was re-elected."[B]

On 1 July Judson, Hileman, and the others got "a very early start & two miles out we pass Redfield at a Ranche & considerable Indian village - He passes us again on his pony during the morning & reaches the fort a short time before us." Judson crossed the Platte on a skiff to Fort Laramie, picks up mail, and while at the sutler's store "we learn that a party of Dragoons are sent to arrest Hileman - When we reach the river we find our wagon on the way down to the ferry with four or five of the company along under arrest - Joe, Jack & Hileman - We are told to go back to the fort & not come over the river - The soldiers & men then proceeded to get the wagon across to the fort & tried to swim the mules but succeeded with only one."[J]

They all went to General Gray who sent them to Capt Harrington who the General appointed Provost Marshal for settling the dispute. They were given the run of the post on Hileman's word that they would appear before Harrington the next morning. They "went to bed when the Soldiers did - Thus ended a very remarkable day & left us where we never dreamed of being in Uncle Sam's garrison & a part of us prisoners" and the others all witnesses.[J]

They are up early on 2 July and have breakfast with the noncommissioned officers. Joe Manning went over the Platte and brought back those needed for the hearing. After the soldier's morning parade they were summoned before the Captain.

The examination now going on the Gen'l & several other officers being present - The taking of evidence takes the bal of the forenoon & before dinner all are without hesitation acquitted - The charge against Hileman was the taking of the forcible possession of his property & moving it under his protest (Redfield's) - Against Jack & Joe was for threatening lynching & sticking a picket pin into his grey mule "Tom."[J]

The decision was to divide the property with Hileman retaining three mules—Redfield taking one and the wagon. The provisions and property were equally divided and Redfield paid Hileman $23 for Judson's prepaid passage. But it was all done under protest. Redfield "does not like the verdict & finds himself worse off than when he came here - I think His reputation here has suffered severely,"[J]

Redfield was left at Fort Laramie "in anything but an amiable mood & dissatisfied with everything even himself - He has to thank the regular officers who agree with him in his secession sympathy for what he has got or that he has anything left."[J]

Joe Manning, "Jack" Humphrey, and Henry Ryerly had the wagon ready and with their newly arranged team of six "were soon off in good style & spirits - We find plenty of sympathizers among the immigrants & Ranchmen - All agreeing - that summary justice should have been administered to Red without permitting him to go to the fort at all."[J]

Independence Day, 1862 Judson's party camped "near a small lake with a party of 6 wagons mostly from Wisconsin headed by Capt Bristol - We think of joining them for the bal of the trip. Evening - We have just had a meeting of our whole force & concluded to join the company mentioned above under Capt Bristol - Manning makes some demurs but finally falls in & we are agreed & off we go together - We close the day with the singing of the old "Star Spangled Banner.""[J]

One day Bristol "came up with a fine-looking train, whose animals, like ours, were nearly all horses or mules, and which traveled at about the same gait. We camped together that night beside a small lake. There was a proposition to join forces. The

Wagon Train Chronology–1862

	Date	Party/Train
Start	March	Bristol Party, Ripon, Wisconsin
"	22 April	McClung, Wapelo, IA
"	27 April	Gould, Mitchell or Chickasaw Co, IA
"	14 May	McComas
Omaha	20 May	McClung
	22 May	Kennedy Train (Scotts)
"	16-28 May	Gould
"	2 June	McComas
"	4 June	Wilson Train chose captain (Gould)
"	5 June	Judson, Hileman & Redfield depart
"	9 June	Sprott, Ryerly, Humphrey join Judson
"	16 June	Crawford
Fort Laramie	22 June	Kennedy Train
"	26 June	Wilson Train (Gould)
"	1-3 July	Judson, Hileman party less Redfield
	4 July	Judson, Hileman party join Bristol Party
	14 July	Crawford
Scott-Young/	7-8 July	Kennedy Train (McClung & Scotts)
Devil's Gate	10 July	Wilson Train (Gould)
"	14 July	Bristol Train (Judson)
McGraw grave	10 July	Kennedy Train (McClung & Scotts)
"	17 July	Bristol Train (Judson)
"	27 July	McComas
South Pass	13 July	Kennedy Train
"	14 July	Wilson Train join Walker Train
"	19-20 July	Bristol Train (Judson)
"	21 July	McComas
"	3-7 August	Crawford
Moran grave,	23 July	Kennedy Train
killed 18 July	26 July	Wilson-Walker Train (Gould)
"	27 July	Jack Train (McComas)
"	12 August	Crawford
Elizabeth Paul	27 July	Kennedy Train
died, age 32	28 July	Wilson-Walker Train (Gould)
"	29 July	Bristol Train (Judson)

Wagon Train Chronology–1862   (Compiled by Author.)

	Date	Party/Train
City of Rocks	3 August	Methodist Party?
City of Rocks	6 August	Salmon River packers
East if Ft Hall	8 August	California miners attacked
"	6 August	Bristol Train (Judson)
City of Rocks	8 August	Smith Train
City of Rocks	9 August	Iowa Train
East if Ft Hall	9 August	Five Denver miners killed
"	10 August	Jack Train (McComas)
"	25 August	Crawford
Fort Hall	7 August	Kennedy Train
"	8 August	Bristol Train (Judson)
"	13 August	Jack Train (McComas)
"	27 August	Crawford
MR 2 Attacks	9 August	Iowa City, Adams, Bristol, Kennedy Trains
Pursue Indians	10 August	Bristol, Kennedy Trains
"	16 August	Jack Train (McComas)
"	31 August	Crawford
Raft River	11 August	Bristol, Kennedy, Walker Trains
"	1 September	Crawford
City of Rocks	15 August	Walker Train
Rock Creek	19–20 August	Bristol, Kennedy Trains
"	6 September	Crawford
Bruneau	28 August	Bristol, Kennedy Trains
"	1 September	Jack or Carseley
"	15 September	Crawford
Leave Bruneau	3 September	Bristol, Kennedy, Jack or Carseley Trains
Owyhee	10 September	Bristol, Kennedy, Jack or Carseley Trains
"	24 September	Crawford
City of Rocks	12 September	15 California Miners attacked
Burnt River	13 September	Bristol, Kennedy, Jack or Carseley Trains
Auburn	18 September	Bristol, Kennedy, Jack or Carseley
"	2 October	Crawford
Walla Walla	27 September	Kennedy Train
"	14 October	Crawford

Wagon Train Chronology–1862 (cont.).

captains of both trains resigned, and the companies resolved to become one train and to choose a captain." The Reverend Sherlock Bristol was again re-elected, almost unanimously. He made them a brief address in which he outlined his "policy as to guarding stock, compactness in traveling, defense of the corral, settlements of quarrels, treatment of friendly Indians, and keeping the Sabbath. It apparently gave good satisfaction "[B]

Judson's old party started "under our new Capt but find that their rules & regulations differ very little from ours."[J] "If any hesitated in assenting to the new regime they were quite won over the next day, when they saw" Captain Bristol[B]

take a horse, about mid-afternoon, and riding ahead out of sight, select a fine camp, where was water and grass, and a good place for defence. This was my usual custom, and I generally went alone. The danger was often great, and I feared to send another, who might not be as good a shot as myself, or as quick to discover danger and avoid it. My company used to congratulate themselves on the excellent camps I selected. These were in striking contrast with those of other trains, which often tied up to the sage bushes, with no water or grass for the stock, their captains, none of them, daring to take the risks I ran daily.[B]

The affairs of Judson's little family were somewhat changed as they had Hileman's three mules harnessed with the other party's three mules making a team that could not be beat. "We go along easily - with mutual dispositions to aid & live in peace & can now give or take jokes without fear of offending - Our Capt is a Congregational Clergyman & we also have another in the party the Rev. Mr. Walcott - a fine appearing elderly man so we shall not want for a monitor to watch our morals or for good examples for our conduct."[J]

Three

To South Pass

On 4 July the Kennedy ox train reached Independence Rock. Robert Scott wrote that they had to stop at noon and camp near there on the Sweetwater River to "bury one of our company, Mr. Geo. Bove, from Batavia, Wapello county." Hamilton Scott recorded the name as "Bovee"—James S. McClung also spelled it that way and that the Bovees were from Jefferson County, Iowa.

According to the Scotts, his death was accidental and a very sad affair. He and one or two other men were out hunting wolves in the bluffs 2–4 miles from the train. Bovee shot a wolf, which fell down a crevice between the rocks. When Bovee went up to it and stooped over to scalp the animal, his revolver in the scabbard which swung from his neck tipped out and the hammer struck a rock, shooting him through the heart. The two men came to him quickly, but he lived only a few minutes. He only could say, "Take care of my family," and was dead.[HS RS]

Thomas Mackay, the man who was with him, went running to the train about four miles away and related the accident. Captain Kennedy sent one of his horse teams which he hitched to a spring wagon and brought Bovee in. The train moved on a couple of miles to Independence Rock where he was buried. Bovee left a wife and two children. "Poor woman, it will be hard for her." The captain put Thomas Mackay to care for the Bovees and drive their ox team.[HS RS]

Robert Scott recorded, "Our train has increased from our original 52 wagons to 80 wagons now, and have 334 people and 532 head of stock. Another train joined us some days ago. We are now better equipped to take care of any Indian raids."[RS]

About four in the afternoon on 6 July the Kennedy Train passed two camped trains who informed them of a murder committed that day.[HS] Alvin Zaring noted:

> This party was from Pikes Peak mines on their way to Powder River mines in Oregon. A man by the name of Young and one by the name of Scott were travelling together with a party of about three wagons. Young and Scott had a quarrel about their team. This dispute was settled between themselves. Young was encouraged by one of the other men to follow him and kill him. So they overtook Scott and Young shot him and killed him. Young shot him from the back of the wagon in which he was riding. They buried him in a three-foot hole in the dust without a box.[1]

The following day the Kennedy Train started at sunrise, drove four or five miles and found tolerable grass on Sweetwater river bottom. Several small trains were camped there. There was lots of grass so the Kennedy Train drove in and stopped too. After they got settled in camp, some from another train came and informed them that the murderer was camped there. "They asked our Captain Kennedy to take charge of the case as they were not strong enough to carry on." Kennedy ordered out twenty well armed men from his train, surrounded Young, and took him prisoner.[HS JM]

Robert Scott remembered, "They formed a court, a judge, lawyers and 12 jury men and had a regular fair trial."[RS] His brother Hamilton recorded, "With a court organized and a jury of twelve men selected, he was given a fair trial and a twelve [eleven] to one verdict, guilty of willful murder. The prisoner kept under guard, we hitched up at two p.m. and drove eight miles."[HS] In James McClung's journal, they "traveled on expecting to deliver him into the hands of the soldiers. So towards night we camped near a company" of the 6th Ohio Cavalry. The soldiers were stationed there to take care of Indians.[RS JM]

"Captain Kennedy called in some of the soldiers."[RS] They had no authority in this civilian matter. A large train was also camped there. "Captain Kennedy called their whole company together and laid the case before them." Apprised of the previous trial and the guilty verdict, this train determined the sentence—the prisoner was to be executed.[HS RS]

The next morning, 8 July, R. Young was given the choice of hanging or shooting. He preferred to be shot. "Said he was sorry for his deed." Twenty-five armed men marched him out a half mile from the train to where his grave had been dug. He was stood by the grave and Captain Kennedy ordered ready, fire. Fourteen of the guns were loaded with bullets and the rest were blanks, none knew which had or had not. "When the signal was given they all fired, the prisoner falling backwards and dying within one minute. It was a sad sight to look upon. We immediately laid him in his grave without even a rough box." "This delayed us so long we stayed in camp and let the cattle graze and rest."[HS RS]

Two days later, there were "two other trains in camp here tonight, making about 200 wagons in all. Also about 150 soldiers here to protect emigrants from Indians which are hostile and lots of them. Our train has been lucky not to have had much Indian troubles so far, which we are thankful for.

We think one reason is because there are so many of us together and we are careful where we camp and watch out."[RS]

John Hileman and Judson were in advance of the Bristol Train on 8 July when they caught a runaway horse. They returned the horse to its owner who belonged to a party of four wagons. Ten of their "men will join us for safety tonight." Judson learned "of further Indian difficulties The killing of 15 men - taking their stock - taking 135 head of horses from some Cal. emigrants etc. etc. ..."[J] The next day they passed a "train of 4 cattle teams & also leave behind the 4 teams mentioned yesterday they having stopped for night - camp nearly an hour before we did - Guess they don't like our society - Very Well I think we can get along without them quite as well as they can without us They have four ponies which a fellow left & ran away from when hollered at - Supposed to have been stolen by him farther up the river."[J]

There was a telegraph station at this place and "usually a ferry - It is now out of order & we had no communication with the other side - About the middle of the afternoon we pass a Frenchmans Lodge - Who confirms all previous Indian reports save the killing of 15 men. He says keep a sharp look & you will not be molested."[J]

Later that day the Bristol Train crossed two bridges to avoid sand hills. "The tollman at the bridge frightens us with stories of Indian depredations - Their determination to take all the horses & mules that offer to pass them - passing the cattle unharmed - of the inability of the soldiers to do anything with them - Of the Indians daring them to fight & of there being some 30 soldiers missing - supposed to be killed"[J]

Soon after breakfast the next morning, "a man from the station above rides by in search of a mule - He says the trouble is greatly exaggerated & that the Stages are running through again regularly - Cheering news surely ..."[J] They met a party of Californians "who said we would be humbugged at Salmon River - They eased our minds on the score of Indians having seen but one solitary Indian this side of Salt Lake - They had seen the grave of the 2 men who were killed but who would not have been had they not first killed an Indian."[J]

The next day, 11 July, Judson in the Bristol Train was "overtaken by 4 teams who say they left Omaha on the 10th June - 5 days after us ... They conclude to join us & so we now have 15 teams about 53 men & feel quite strong."[J]

The following day they passed Devil's Gate and Independence Rock. "Have seen no Indians yet & are beginning to think we shall not see any   We have been in sight of an immense train of cattle teams nearly all the PM ..."[J]   Sherlock Bristol:

> Leaving the Platte, we went up the Sweetwater. On our way we were met by fugitives fleeing toward the settlements from Indian raids all along the overland stage route.   They had stopped the stages, killed passengers and drivers, robbed and burned the stations, and had driven off the relays of horses and mules. We met soldiers rushing away in fear, and their officers commanded us to retreat also. We heard their stories and went on.[B]

On 15 July the Bristol Train "met a lone Californian on foot this am   He says we'll have no trouble with the Indians - pass more deserted Ranches & Stations ... We pass today too the graves of 2 men probably 12 miles apart" which were those of George Scott and R. Young.[J]

The next day, "Having seen several suspicious characters today & learning that we are camped on the identical spot where the two men were killed by the Sioux - we increase our guard tie our stock to the wagon wheels & prepare for any emergency."[J]   The following morning, the 17th, "On the top of the hill near half a mile long we find the grave of the two men murdered by the Indians with this inscription on both head &

foot board "James McGraw & brother in law from Ill. were killed by the Indians June 28th, 1862 and his wife taken by them   Beware of Indians."[1]

Oliver B. Slater was fourteen when he left Garden Grove, Iowa, on 12 May 1862 "headed for the West. Our train consisted of seven wagons, drawn by mules and horses. Two of the wagons belonged to my Father and Mother. We traveled along until we reached the Missouri River on May nineteenth. There we fell in with twenty-nine more wagons from Iowa, Wisconsin, and New York." They left Ice Springs on the Sweet Water on 1 July.[2]

> On Sage Creek the Shoshone Indians attacked the rear of our train, cutting off one wagon belonging to men from Illinois. The wagon upset on one. They took his own axe and cut his head open. The other man they had driven back about a quarter of a mile. They shot him with three arrow in the shoulder and two through his body, and shot one eye with a bullet; then cut the harness off the team and took the horses. They tried to cut off one four horse team driven by a woman, but she whipped up her team and got ahead of them. The train was corralled at the foot of the hill while part of the men went back and brought in the two that were killed, which we buried in one grave.[3]

They left camp at dusk and drove ten miles to Antelope Springs where they arrived at midnight. There they found thirty wagons. Slater remembered, "At this time these same Shoshone Indians were burning stage stations and killing passengers and drivers on the Overland Road between Green River and Denver. They had driven off 300 head of stock belonging to the Overland toll road."[4]

One evening Bristol, not twenty rods from camp, "found a fresh dug grave. A rough board at its head informed us that there the Indians had attacked their train, killed several, and that two women and their children had been captured and carried off! ... Our men rested uneasily that night. Few of us slept. We were thinking of the sad fate of those wives and children!"[B]

The Kennedy Train had passed here a week before Bristol, on 10 July. McClung: "On top of the hill we passed a grave. The inscription on the head reads as follows, 'two persons named Mcgraw who was Brotherinlaws was killed by the indians on the 28th of June, 1862' ... About 2 o'clock we camped near Antelpe Springs by the South Pass post office."[JM]

The Wilson Train had been camping at the same sites as the Walker Train for several days. On 14 July, near South Pass, they joined Captain John P. Walker's Train.[G]

The Bristol Train came through the Pass on the 18th. Here they would leave the telegraph and stage route. An army post was there with the famous mountain man, Jim Bridger, who was a scout for the Army. Bristol and others passing by got advice from Bridger about the route ahead and Indian difficulties. William Smedley who was originally heading for the Idaho Salmon River gold mines decided to change his destination to Oregon.[5] Judson and others learned the "unpleasant item that we must go from Ft. Hall to Ft. Wallawalla."[J] The next day

> We are joined by 5 wagons 9 men 4 ladies & a baby from the large train which will make one train when Meeker comes up tomorrow 20 wagons - 7 Women - 2 babies - about 50 men & 60 head of stock - Among the acquisitions are a Mr. Root with another mans wife - They had travelled together several days in the large train - the husband & wife had a falling out - husband took a girl from the train & started for Salt Lake with the train while Root with the wife came with us - Comment is unnecessary [J]

Sunday 20 July Judson recorded a census of the Bristol Train. "Early in the am Meeker & Co come up & we also have another addition to our train which probably will not again change till we reach Ft. Hall & stands thus - 22 teams & about 60 men - A very good train - large enough & not too large."[J]

A day later, the 21st, Evans McComas "Had an introduction to old Bridger. He gave us a description of the road to Fort Hall via Lander's Cutoff. Come 12 miles, fell in with & formed into a company of 16 wagons, with a Denver company. We number about 35 men. Elected Wm. Jack as Capt. Come along the base of the Wind River Mountains."[EM]

A steady procession of emigrant wagon trains on the overland trail passed over the Continental Divide through South Pass in 1862. Some emigrants followed the older route of the Oregon Trail, through the southwest corner of Wyoming and through Soda Springs, Idaho. Oliver B. Slater traveled this route and arrived at Soda Springs about 15 July.

> We were just coming in to camp, the teams ahead were unhitched and turned out to graze, when the Indians came down the creek as though they were coming to camp. When near the camp they turned toward the horses and began shaking their robes and stampeded nineteen head. The man with the horses commenced to shooting at them. They returned the fire but no one was hurt. Some were hobbled with leather and some with shackles made of iron. The leather hobbles were cut off by the Indians while the horses were running. The others they had to leave. We could see the Indians driving the horses up the mountain, but did not dare follow them. I saw one, Smith, that pretended to be a great Indian fighter, crawl in the wagon and hide.[6]

17,000 Shoshoni
Approximate numbers in mid–1800s

Eastern Shoshoni (Western Wyoming)   1840 **3,000**
    Several bands under Chief Washakie   2,000
                             1850s 1,200

Northern Shoshoni (Central & Southern Idaho & Northern Utah.)   **5,000**
    Bannocks (Descendants of Northern Paiutes who migrated to east.)   **800**
    (Co-existing mainly with Fort Hall Shoshoni, a few with the Lemhi)
    Fort Hall Shoshoni (East Snake River Plain)   1850s 1,000
    Northwestern Shoshoni   1,500
    (10 bands in Northern Utah and SE Idaho)
    Bruneau Shoshoni (Bruneau Valley; Owyhee County)   350
    Boise Shoshoni (Boise, Payette, Weiser Valleys) 1840s 1,000+
    (Boise Valley)   late 1850s 300
    Lemhi Shoshoni (Lemhi Valley)   1,800
    Mountain Shoshoni   several hundred
    (Sheepeaters & Upper Weiser, across Central Idaho into Wyoming)

Western Shoshoni   **9,000**
(West of Great Salt Lake to Winnemucca, NV & from Owyhee Co, ID south thru eastern and Central NV)
    Gosiutes   900
    11 Shoshoni bands across Northern Nevada   8,145
    Southern or Panamint Shoshoni   small number

8,000 Northern Paiute

11 bands (Central & SE Oregon and Western Nevada)   1860s **8,000**

The Shoshoni Indians.   (Compiled by Author).

Sources: *Handbook of North American Indians,* William C. Sturtevant, ed, *Vol. 11: Great Basin,* Volume ed, Warren L. D'Azevedo (Washington DC: Smithsonian Institution, 1986); Brigham D. Madsen, *Shoshoni Frontier and the Bear River Massacre* (Salt Lake City: University of Utah Press, 1985); Madsen, *Chief Pocatello: The 'White Plume'* (Salt Lake City: University of Utah Press, 1986).

The next morning seven wagons had to be left in the camp because of the lost horses. Those who no longer had a wagon were taken in by the others. About three days later Slater and "two friends stopped to pick currants by the roadside. In about ten minutes we came out and saw five Indians a half mile behind us on horseback coming right after us, and maybe you think we didn't run. They drove us to the wagons, then they disappeared into the brush."[7]

]   The Lander Road   [

There was this heavy traffic of wagons on the Lander Cutoff too. Some trains had passed ahead of those who's accounts we are following.

Heavy Indian depredation was encountered at the crossing of Green River and continued across the Snake River Plain. In this area it was not just Indians who were continually attempting and succeeding in stampeding the emigrant stock, but "Jayhawkers" too. This term had come into being at the outbreak of the Civil War with the bloody fighting in Missouri and on the Kansas border. In this locale these "Jayhawkers" could also be termed "Renegade White Men," as a renegade is one who turns against their own kind. They were murderous thieves, preying on the emigrants who were chasing after lost, stolen, or stampeding stock.

The morning of 20 July the Kennedy Train was missing an ox. "Thomas Paul and A. Hunter started on the search for him."[HS] They were at the second crossing of the Green River. That evening the Kennedy Train bought an emigrant ferry boat for five dollars. Two days later, "All ferried over by ten o'clock and our men came in with the lost ox about that time."[HS]

The Bristol Train was first crossing the Green River when another train "lost 5 head of horses - a small party tracked them for 12 miles & discovered the camp of the thieves - white men - They came back & 40 men started out in pursuit in the hope of surrounding the party numbering about 12." The next day, "The party in pursuit of the horse thieves has returned unsuccessful - They followed them far toward Mormondom - a significant fact from which we all draw the same inference."[J]

At the second branch of Green River Bristol bought a ferry boat, probably the same one the Kennedy Train had used but for more money. After the train was across the river, Bristol then sold the boat for five dollars less to the train behind.[B] "The party to whom we sold the boat & whom we left crossing were probably careless and neglected their watch as they lost all their cattle & all their horses & mules but 5 or 6 by a stampede - The occasion they dont know but probably by Indians or renegade white men."[J]

A few days later, on the 26th, the Jack Train crossed their wagons on the ferry and "came near getting one man drowned … Here we left 5 of our men who bought the ferry."[EM] McComas noted:

This is where a great deal of depredations have been committed by Indians & white Jayhawkers on the emigrants. We will here keep a sharp lookout. This evening a party of 5 men from another train came to us with the ferrryman who crossed us over the river. They had taken them prisoners thinking them to be horse thieves as their horses had been stampeded the night before. They proved their innocence by men in our train who were acquainted with them & will travel with us a few days. Their names were Waters and John McGavern.[EM]

July 27: This morning we heard the firing of about 100 guns which we thought was from a train attacked by Indians. Come 2 miles and saw a band of Indians &

white men cross the road ahead of us. As they appeared to be tired we now suppose the firing to be from a fight between two companies of Jayhawkers. Come 8 miles to Bear Creek. Here is the grave of a man killed by Indians. There was a fight here in which two more white men were badly wounded.[EM]

Evans McComas noted later, on 16 August, that "Martin Moran was the name of the first man that we came to that had been killed by Indians. We was one days drive west of Green River."[EM]

William Smedley later wrote, "On the Lander Road, 'Moran of Illinois' killed by arrows while after stolen horses."[8] McClung, "passed the grave of Matan Moarn that was killed here by the Indians the 18th of this month. The dead was from Miss. bound for the Salmon river mines"[JM] The Kennedy Train passed there on the 22th, "Saw some squads of Indians at a distance. We put out picket guards tonight. The Indians have been attacking the emigrants and stealing stock along here. They killed one man a day or two ago. His grave is close by our camp tonight."[HS] As Alvin Zaring passed by, Moran's "little dog was lying on the lonely grave."[9]

The next day the Kennedy Train "Drove only two miles before dinner and stopped where several small trains are camped. Their stock was stampeded last night by Indians, but they got them back today. Their cattle was inside the corral of wagons, but they broke through, smashed up some wagons and hurt two men badly."[RS]

That day the Bristol Train was still at a branch of the Green River. "The train across the river lost two horses last night by Indians or thieves the lariats being cut & the horses gone - Guess they had a sleepy guard - We have a report of 2 men who were hunting stock on foot with three more on horseback being killed by the Indians on Friday last not far from here -

The horsemen got away while the footmen were surrounded and shot to death with arrows."[J]

The Walker Train passed Moran's grave on the 26th, the day before McComas did. "Started early this morning and as we went up the hill found we had staid all night on the ground where the Indians had taken some horses from some emigrants who in trying to recover them one man lost his life and two others were severely wounded, his grave is on the left side of the road as you go up the hill. He was killed on the 18th of July 1862."[G]

Bringing up the rear of the emigration, on the 11th of August Captain Crawford's escort and emigrants "reached New Fork of Green river ... on the 12th all the emigrants were over. Here we found the first evidence of Indian depredations —a grave, from the inscription on which we learned that Patrick Moran, of Missouri, was killed by Indians on the 18th of July, and two men wounded."[10]

The cattle of the Kennedy Train were stampeded twice on the night of the 24th.[RS]   Two night's later their cattle were stampeded again, at about eleven o'clock, losing one hundred and fifty. The next day, Sunday the 27th, some of the stock were still nearby so they recovered all but fifteen.[HS]   They remained in camp all day. Mrs. Thomas Paul was pregnant and had been ill for some time. She died in childbirth about nine in the morning, but the baby survived. She was buried in the "evening in a pretty open place by a Pine Fir tree in the mountains, and put a fence around the grave, and a marker in the side of the tree."[RS]

Ten of the men started out the next morning to hunt for the fifteen cattle which were still missing. That night the cattle they had were left "in their yokes and chained to trees. They kept snorting and trying to get away all night. The Indians were sneaking around, but we could not see them. Every body was afraid. We had men pickets hiding out in the timber watching. This was a wild night."[RS]   The men who went to look for the missing cattle returned about ten o'clock. "Found four head of the cattle, that leaves some eight head that we will never get."[HS] Alvin Zaring added:

> In the stampede, the cattle went north of the camp. About one mile from the camp, a large grizzly bear got after them which caused them to run over a very rough mountainous country for about fifteen miles. We did not realize how perilous the undertaking to regain the cattle was as the Indians were exceedingly hostile in this part of the country. We arrive in camp about eleven p.m. with four head of cattle. After we had travelled about three hundred miles another train overtook us, returning the rest of the stock which had wandered back on the road.[11]

That day the Walker Train passed the thirty six wagons of the Kennedy Train "who have been camped for some time here in the mountains, they have had their cattle stampeded four or five times, there was a woman died in their train yesterday, she left six children and one of them only two days old, poor little thing it had better have died with its mother, they made a good picket fence around the grave. This same train had a man accidentally shot down at Independence Rock, they seem to be very unfortunate."[G]

The next day, 29 July, the Bristol Train, behind on the trail, passed "this afternoon a beautiful grave made in an opening in the forest & directly beneath a fine fir tree - Twas made on the 27th inst (only 2 days ago) & was enclosed in a picket yard of hewn timber - A board set into a notch sawed into the tree informed us that the grave contained the remains of Mrs. Elizabeth Paul - aged 32 years - beneath some kind friend had pinned a paper on which were written 3 beautiful & appropriate verses."[J]

That same day the Walker Train "passed a grave on the side of a mountain, it was the grave of a man that was supposed to have been killed by the Indians, there was an arrow with blood on the point lying beside the grave, he was only buried about six inches under ground, the Maple Train ahead of us opened the grave, he had a bullet hole through his temple, they found another new grave a little way from that back in the woods, this is the place of all places for the doing of foul deeds, with its deep ravines and gorges and thick forests." [G]

The next day the Jack Train, passed this "grave of a man who had been murdered or killed by Indians & buried by a train ahead of us."[EM] That day too, in the Bristol Train:

Mr. Ives this morning found a half mile up the mountain from our camp a plain trail made by horses & mules running along a high ridge - He also found strong evidences of foul play committed by Indians or white men far meaner - There were pieces of harness - a horse collar - a new unsoiled pr of boots - Moulds wrench etc for a navy revolver - 3 powderhorns - a brass spur & various other things - Had we have known of the discovery in time we should have sent out a party for further search - Three or four miles beyond we found beside the road a grave - on which was nailed a paper stating that Mr. Carariaghs Co had opened the same on the 27th thinking to recognize the corpse as some acquaintance gone before & had found a body only six inches under ground - unknown - with a bullet hole in his temple - an arrow about the grave - a bloody shirt etc. - Twas so far decayed as to be immovable appeared to be a man of 50 yrs of age - This man was evidentally murdered & probably the murder was connected with the transaction by which the things Ives found were left - I am satisfied twas white men did the deed.[J]

For about three weeks after Crawford passed Moran's grave at no time were any Indians to be seen. "The next grave was on La Barge Creek, in the Bear River Mountains, on the head-board of which was the following: 'Opened by Kavanaugh's train on the 27th of July, 1862. The body of a man found too badly decayed for removal. One shot in the temple and an arrow shot. Supposed to have been killed by Indians.'"[12]

Henry R. Herr of York, Pennsylvania was traveling with a Mr. Chamberlain.   At Fort Laramie they had joined other emigrants traveling with the government escort train.   Captain Crawford had them passing this grave on the 15th, but Herr's journal entry was the 16th, with a different death date:

Passed the graves of several persons. With following inscription on one, "The deceased was a man about 50 years old; was found dead Aug. 2nd, '62; a bullet ball passing through his bead and poisoned arrow in his breast. Killed by Indians." ... Saw several bears both grizzly and black. They often dig up the dead bodies.[13]

FOUR

Miners Killed

The Bristol Train did not travel on Sundays and on 3 August Judson noted, "We must have had in the space of a mile at least 100 wagons last night." He mostly referred to the Kennedy Train as "The Newbern Colony." That train, "which camped about a mile from us & the train Shannon is with have rolled on today."[J] The evening before Bristol invited the Kennedy Train

> to stay with us over Sabbath and attend the preaching service, which I held in our corral every Sabbath. They partly agreed to do so. But when the morning came they moved on as usual. They had not proceeded far, before an unaccountable panic seized upon nearly every animal in the train. It was the noted "stampede," so often spoken of by travelers in connection with migrations across the Western plains.[B]

Judson and Bristol had the stampede occurring on 3 August. Hamilton and Robert Scott and Jane Gould had the events as occurring on the 2nd. Between eleven and twelve o'clock a loose horse belonging to another train run up by some ox teams. The cattle have had the jitters more than a week. Scare at anything. We think they smell the Indians. The horse scared the cattle as he ran by them. The cattle give a big snort and away they went, tails up. About 25 teams ran away, upset wagons, ran over men, women and children and jumped over each other and scattered everything over the rocky roads and over high banks. Hurt a lot of people, some very seriously. It was a terrible mixup.[RS]

Mrs. Townsend from Monroe, Iowa was dangerously wounded and died the next afternoon from being run over. Wilson Scott from Fremont had a leg broken. Mrs. Hoover's head was bruised.[RS HS]

Mr. Hoover had body injuries and 32 others bruised, sprained and scratched, Wagons badly broken, etc. It was the worst mess ever, I can't describe it. We had to travel a while with only two oxen on a wagon to be able to handle them, they are so badly scared. The cattle we loosened from the wagons were still in the yokes and chained together. They would hist their tails and snort every 20 or 30 minutes and try to get away. We had to keep them away from those hitched to the wagons to keep them from running away again.[RS]

Jane Gould referred to the Kennedy Train as the Canada Train. The day following the stampede, "We did not get a very early start this morning on account of our hard day's drive yesterday ... We hear the Canada train have had another stampede." Thomas Pauls infant had died the night before. Late in the afternoon the Wilson Train passed by the Kennedy Train who [G] had just buried the babe of the woman who died a few days ago, and were just digging a grave for another woman ... she was run over by the cattle and wagons when they stampeded yesterday. She lived twenty-four hours ... She leaves a little two year old girl and a husband, they say he is nearly crazy with sorrow ... After cattle have been frightened once or twice there is no safety with them. Yesterday there were several loose horses came running up when the train of cattle started pellmell, crippled two men besides killing the woman. They mark nearly half their camps with dead cattle. I never supposed that cattle would run so in yoke and hitched to a wagon.[G]

Then next day, the Bristol Train passed the "grave containing the body of a Woman killed by a stampede of cattle teams belonging to the Newbern Colony which left our camp yesterday morning - It also contained the corpse of a babe left by the woman Mrs. Paul whose grave beneath the fir tree has been before described."[J]

That day the Kennedy Train's cattle were "still upset and nervous, this a.m. but we hitched up and will keep the teams quite aways apart and watch them carefully. We got along very well with cattle today. No trouble. Camped tonight on a branch of Snake River."[RS] Hamilton Scott, "Our cattle being so unsafe to travel all together, we divided the company into four parts and travelled some distance apart all camping together at night. Drove twenty miles and camped on a branch of Snake River."[HS]

Daniel McLaughlin had left Omaha behind on the first of June en route to Salmon River. His train

kept guard over the stock night and day; and as a consequence were never troubled by the Indians at all on the route. They attacked trains in our front and rear, stampeding stock and massacreing the emigrants whenever they found them off their guard. One Indian who could talk pretty good English came into our camp when we were within two days drive of Ft. Hall, who represented himself as a Bannock, and said the Shoshones had followed us 150 miles with a view of making an attack upon us, but said they had given it up, as they found us always prepared.[1]

The next day about three in the afternoon, they "saw a train corralled at the foot of a hill with their animals still hitched to the wagon; conjecturing that all was not right, and noticing considerable commotion below, we descended cautiously, and sure enough found that a party of Indians had attacked them, doing no further damage than the driving off of some of their stock. A party started in pursuit and espied them in a ravine in the act of dressing a cow they had just killed, and cautiously crept to within pistol shot and then simultaneously fired killing eight and wounding several others."[2]

]   California Miners Attacked   [

The Bristol Train were some 20 miles east of Fort Hall, on 6 August, when they "met this eve a party of packers from Cal who give a very discouraging report of the Salmon river mines - Don't think they know as much about them as we do."[3] Bristol:

One evening we were met by eight miners returning homeward to the States. Each had two mules; one he rode, the other carried his clothes, provisions, blankets, and perhaps his gold. We invited them to share the hospitalities of our camp. They staid with us over night and gave us much valuable information, as to our route and the mines. They were fine fellows. They left us early the next morning. As my train was about to start, I took my station as usual some distance ahead, holding the foremost back till the last wagon was in line, for I never allowed my train to stretch out in unreasonable length. Hence no stragglers were captured from our train. While waiting and looking over the adjacent hills, I discovered the upper half of an Indian's head looking down upon us. Looking steadily at it, it slowly sunk down like that of a partridge till it was out of sight. I knew what was up. So bidding the train move on, I stood still, gun in hand, and as each wagon passed me I called out one of its armed men and when the last went by, I had about forty at my side. The Indians finding they were discovered soon appeared on their ponies and rode back and forth on the hillside at the top of their speed. They made threatening gestures but were careful to keep out of reach of our rifle balls. They ransacked our camp ground for plunder, and the last we saw of them they were taking our back track, and making haste to overtake the eight miners who had left us half an hour before. We knew they would be overtaken, and probably all be slain![B]

This was on Thursday, 7 August, the Bristol Train, was a little east of Fort Hall. Judson added:

Soon after we leave camp this morning we discover a small party of Indians on a neighboring hill looking down with greedy eyes upon the 3 or 4 lazy teams still in camp - We halted & sent back for the teams & they came & they came up in a hurry - As soon as we were out of way, they paid the campground a visit - on their ponies which had till now been kept out of sight - They followed us at a respectful distance to where an Ox

train had been in camp & we saw no more of them -
We drove through the dust till we overtook the Ox
trains & camped for noon to avoid their dust.[J]

Both Judson and Bristol were correct in surmising that the
California miners would be attacked, but got them mixed up
with five Denver miners who were killed in another party. The
Bristol Train later learned about the attack on the California
miners, on 1 September. While encamped on the Bruneau
River they were joined by a small wagon train which had in
their company some of the "Packers whom we met on the 6th
Aug & who two days later had been attacked by Indians - 5 of
their no. wounded - 13 of their horses killed & 3 with their
packs taken off by the Indians - They fought them for 3 hours
& proved themselves brave fellows."[B]

William Purvine, later on Powder River, obtained differing
information about these miners as he confused the miners from
California using pack animals with the wagon train of miners
from Denver. "I am just furnished with a list of men wounded,
35 miles east of Fort Hall, out of a party of seven, on their way
from California for the States, in an engagement with Indians.
None of the party were killed. They lost all their pack animals
and saved nothing but their arms and ammunition they had on
their persons. They succeeded in killing and wounding a
considerable number of the Indian. The names of those
wounded are: John Bluebaker. Pennsylvania; John Dobkins,
Iowa; Ebin Brour, Ohio; Geo. Metcalf, Illinois; Henry Martin,
Ill. One or two of these are dangerously wounded, but are here
doing well."[3]

The day of the attack on the California miners, 8 August,
one of the men of McComas' party, with Captain Jack, and two
others started for Fort Hall in advance of the train. Out some
eight miles they found an Indian who they supposed to be a
scout. They went on and then saw about twenty Indians, so
turned back to the train. Soon after McComas [EM]

saw about 12 men coming to our corral. We got our guns in trim but they proved to be a party of Californians on prospecting tour who had just had a fight with a party of Indians. They had 14 horses shot and also all their packs taken and four men wounded, one shot through the lungs, one through the hips, one through the thigh and one in the knee. We took them in and waited for a Dr. to come up with another train. Bound up their wounds the best as we could. With them and the other train who will probably travel togather, as we will all number about 90 men.^{EM}

]   Five Miners Killed   [

The Virginia City, Nevada *Territorial Enterprise*, on 1 October 1862, reported an encounter.

L.F. Yates, who arrived in Virginia City a few days since from Pike's Peak, has given us the following particulars of a fight his train had on the 8th of last August, about one and a half miles this side of the junction of the Lander's Cut off and Fort Bridger roads. Their train consisted of 15 wagons and 40 men, with a number of women and children. The train was attacked while passing along a ravine by a party of Indians being concealed in among a thick growth of poplar bushes. When the attack commenced, most of the front wagons were some 80 rods in advance. They formed in corral, and entrenched behind their wagons, refused the slightest aid to those who were struggling with the savages in the rear. The party thus left to fight their way through the ambushed Indians numbered but nine men, and there were but four guns with which to maintain the battle.[4]

Yates stated that five of the nine were killed: "Parmlee, James Steele, James A. Hart, Rufus C. Mitchell, from Central City, Colorado Territory, and McMahn, residence unknown." One man, Frank Lyman, was wounded. He was shot through the lungs, but recovered.[5]

William Purvine, later on Powder River, recorded a differing account from that of Yates. Purvine was

> permitted to take from the memorandum of Mr. V.D. Johnson, of Denver, the following facts: Mr. Johnson and party left Denver on the 10th day of July last, for Salmon river mines, and proceeded with great dispatch until within thirty-five miles of Hall, when they were suddenly attacked by a large party of Indians on horseback, and lost, after a severe conflict, the following members of their party:
>
> Killed.—James Steel, of Iowa; Rufus Mitchell, of Stephenson county, Ill.; Jeremiah McMahon, Philadelphia, Pa.; J.A. Hurt, Kent county, Maryland; — Parmlee, Winnegago county, Ill.
>
> Wounded.—Frank Lyman. St. Joseph, Mo.; ball entered the left breast, and passed out under right shoulder—doing well. — Stines, slightly in the face.
>
> The Indians finally, after killing the teams, drove the party from the wagons and carried away all the moveables, including several guns and revolvers, and a considerable quantity of ammunition The Indians seemed to be much excited, and made very awkward work of it, otherwise the whole party would have been murdered. The party killed eight or ten Indians, a part of which number was left on the field, besides a large number they knew to be wounded.[6]

The *Territorial Enterprise* account, according to L.F. Yates, continued:

The 31 men who were hidden snugly behind their wagons, with a single honorable exception, refused to render the slightest assistance to those who were fighting for their lives and the lives of their families so near them. Although they had 27 guns they refused to lend a single gun, when at one time four men went to ask assistance. The cowards all clung to their arms, and lay trembling behind their wagons. A man named Perry, or Berry, was the only one who had sufficient courage to attempt to render his struggling friends any assistance. He was shot in the face before reaching the rear wagons, and was carried back to the corral. The fight lasted nearly two hours, and some seven or eight Indians were killed, as at various times they charged out of the bushes on their ponies. Several Indian horses were killed, and at length the few left alive fought through to where their 30 heroic friends (?) were corralled, leaving the killed and two wagons in possession of the Indians. 30 bigger cowards and meaner men than these above mentioned never crossed the plains. We are certain that every man of them left the States for fear of being drafted into the army.[7]

This attack was on the day following the attack on the California miners. While the Jack Train "laid by" this day, McComas was among eighteen men who

went out to look after the Indians and found 4 men killed and scalped and laying in the road with indications of a hard fight. Their wagon was left, flour, coffee, bacon & laying scattered around. We found a wagon track leading off toward the hills. Followed it about 3 miles & it got so late in the evening that we could not get to the corrall before dark so we could not follow farther as we were afraid that they might attack our train in our absence at night. As we came home saw 15 Indians. I stood guard tonight. The Indians came within 200 yards of the camp. I gave the alarm and aroused the train. They let us alone.[EM]

The next day the Jack Train drove ten miles. "Come to where the men were killed. Took them and put them in the wagon. Brought them up to where we camp, gave them as desent burial as we could."[EM] Judson noted, "The four men were from Denver."[J]

The following day, 11 August, the Jack Train "Drove 6 miles, came to a deep canyon. When our train was fairly in the canyon our scouts came in on the run & reported Indians. G. Walker, Neil Howie" and McComas "with three others took to the rocks to gain the high ground so as to fight them away from the train." When the supposed Indians came up they turned out to be a part of the train of Denver miners who had been attacked. They were "going back with the ferrymen and some friendly Indians to bury the dead."[EM]

Bristol agreed with Purvine on five miners being wounded. He was in agreement with Captain Crawford in stating that four miners were killed. The Crawford Escort within thirty miles of Fort Hall "found the graves of five persons, said to have been killed by Indians on the 9th of August. Some of them had been shot with buckshot, which, with other circumstances, leads me to believe that white men had a hand in this massacre."[8]

Another grave was also found. Henry Herr, "After passing through Canyon some six miles we came across a grave with following inscription 'Unknown man found by Cap't William's Co. Aug 13th and by him interred. Murdered by indians, being shot with buck shot through back of head. His cloths laid on top of the grave.'"[9]

Captain Crawford on the same day, 25 August, passed the graves of:

One unknown man found by Captain Glenn's party August 13. He had been shot in the back of the head with buckshot. Three miles farther there were five graves, side by side, of persons supposed to have been killed by Indians. Rufus C. Mitchell, N. Howie, James Steel, David Whitmer, and Frank Sessions were the names inscribed over them. This was in the vicinity of Fort Hall, and happened on the 9th of August, we passing on the 25th. We learned from the ferryman that while these five men were slain by the Indians twenty armed men from the same train stood upon a hill near by and made no attempt to rescue their comrades. There are strong reasons for believing that white men bore a part in this massacre.[10]

Henry Herr continued his entry for that day, with differing information. Three miles after passing the grave of the unknown man, the Escort Party came to the graves of four more men, "Frank Essex, David Whitmer, James Steel & George Brown, found dead a short distance from the road murdered by indians. Interred by a friend of one of the deceased." The dead were all from Sioux City, Iowa. The Indians "are called the Banneck Indians, and can frequently be seen watching us from top of the mountains through glasses."[11]

Two days later, the 27th, about ten miles east of Fort Hall, Herr recorded, "a man was shot through right shoulder by indians and had several arrows in his back; was found by the Herder of our escourt crawling into camp all his cloths having been taken and left for dead. Some of these are the Snake Indians."[12]

Nearing Fort Hall, McComas "Found it 800 miles to the Salmon River Mines & 200 to Deer Lodge Valley. No body knew where they were going. Some wanted to go to Oregon some to California, some to Wallah Wallah & some to Deer Lodge. Walker & I were for Deer Lodge but could not get our things hauled. Here my friend Neil Howie, Madison, Wisc., left us for Deer Lodge."[EM]

The next day, 13 August, the Jack Train "crossed Port Neuf river on a ferry boat made out of two skiffs. Wounded Californians start for Salt Lake four left us for the States. Eight go on with us, Here also Tom Laven struck for Salt Lake to winter. We go to Wallah Wallah Valley."[EM]

At about 10 o'clock on 6 August James McClung in the Kennedy Train passed opposite the vacant Fort Hall "which is some 6 miles from the road to our right." At 5 o'clock "we camped on a small creek, having traveled 18 miles. Here is some Frenchmen that had Squass for wives, had a traveling post ... Here was a road turned to the right which they told us led to Salmon river mines."[JM] One of the Frenchman traders was probably Johnny Grant, whose father, Richard, was the former Chief Trader at Fort Hall before the Hudson Bay Company closed it in 1855.[*]

George Chandler's "father had no thought of going to Oregon. He was headed for California, but what changed the whole history was the discovery of wonderful gold deposits in the Salmon River" area southeast of Lewiston. "We heard of the unprecedented richness of these mines and decided to go there ... and had come over a new government road called Landers Cutoff ... we heard nothing more of these Salmon River mines until we reached Fort Hall. Here we learned that it was impossible to get to them except on foot, and that supplies were packed in only on the shoulders of men."[13]

The Chandlers decided to head for California again but at Raft River, where the road left the Oregon Trail for California, "a certain Oliver Shinn, whose wife was a sister to my mother ... had started from Denver and was one or two hundred miles ahead of us. He had heard of the gold strike in the Powder River so he wrote a letter and put it into a split stick placed by the road telling my father of these mines, that he was going

*See Volume I, *The Boise Massacre on the Oregon Trail,* 38–41.

there, and urging father to do likewise. My father got this letter and thereby hangs this tale. This is how we happened to come to Baker."[14]

When Daniel McLaughlin reached Fort Hall, "we found a large number there encamped, and for the first time learned that in order to get to Salmon river, we either had to cross the Snake up to ... the Bitter Root Valley ... packing ... miles over Mountains ... distance of about 500 miles—or else follow the Snake River down to Walla Walla, and go from there to the Salmon—a distance of 800 miles."

As the "women were anxious to get somewhere as soon as possible ... Trains commenced dividing up, some taking the shortest route, while others thought the longest way round was the surest way there. To settle the matter with me a man named Young, came into camp that day—direct from Florence via Walla Walla—and brought the news that we were too late. Salmon was a rich thing, a big thing in fact, but like all big things had its limits. The basin where the gold was found was about seven miles long by three wide, and every claim there had been taken early in the Spring. Not less than twenty thousand persons were there when he left, but four-fifths of them were doing nothing. Plenty of claims paid as high as 100 ounces a day to the man while the thing lasted.—But while a hundred or more were making small fortunes every hour, thousands stood around unable to make grub." McLaughlin's party went on toward Walla Walla. More gold strikes were found around "Fabulous Florence."[15]

Days later and about one hundred miles out from Fort Hall, McLaughlin's party

met a party of gold hunters from Florence—who had wintered there—on their way to the States. They confirmed the reported richness of the place, but also said the basin was nearly dug out. One of them, rather an intelligent man, said he had been nine years on the coast, had now made his "pile" and was going home. From him I learned that new discoveries had been made on Pouder River, and on John Day River, that prospected well, and he had some Pouder River dust along, and its exhibition made every one feel anxious to get there.—The mines were being opened when he came through; a town was started and provisions coming in from Walla Walla and Dalles in great abundance. "For Pouder river," now was all the cry.[16]

On Thursday, 7 August, a Mormon trading station was passed by the Bristol Train. They were informed of the Deer Lodge mines, now in Montana, and the traders

insist upon the existence of a good road through to Liet Mullins road & Salmon River - Tell us long stories & try to induce us to go up from here - We camp for the day near their Station - consult upon the subject & vote to go on via Ft. Bois etc. - These Mormons are in wagons & have several wagons & harness brot from above - of course left by men who have been obliged to leave them - It is the impression of some that $5 pr wagon for ferriage - wagons etc is the inducement for urging emigrants to take this Deer Lodge route - we are in sight of the three Butes - singular looking - Tall mountains & probably 30 miles distant We are camped near Shannons train again - A small party of Indians are with their ponies at the station about a mile distant have had a look at them only at a distance [J]

The next day Judson: "leave camp at half past six with the Ox train (Capt Walker) & get mixed with it - All arrive at the ferry of the Port-Neuf together - 8 miles from camp - Our party crosses first & go into noon camp - The stream is 6 to 8 rods wide - not swift - & ten miles distant empties into the

Snake river on the north - The ferry boat is two skiffs with a platform of poles across pulled by a rope stretched across the river - We take two wagons at a time & get over fast swimming the horses" [J]

The ferry men told Judson that "tis 300 miles to Deer Lodge that the diggings are limited & that they have crossed over 300 teams which have turned back from Deer Lodge - That tis but 200 miles from here to Ft. Boise & 416 to Wallawalla & Powder river & Salmon both on the route - We are satisfied we are on the right track & all feel well ... The indians left at the last station have come up & camped on the hill near the ferry" [J]

The Wilson-Walker Train then crossed the Portneuf River paying a dollar and a half for each wagon.

> Here we saw some Shoshone or Snake Indians, there were four or five Mormon wagons here trading, they sold flour to some of the train for ten dollars per hundred. Charley bought a dozen onions, traded some caps for them, they sell them for two cents apiece, they are brought from Salt Lake. We had onion soup for supper, which was very good. The ferrymen were, quite gentlemanly fellows for this part of the world. We took lunch after we crossed the river, then came five miles and camped on a high bank in the sage brush, had to bring water up a very steep bank some distance from the creek. [G]

Later, in a newspaper account, "At this place Charles Bullwinkle had taken a little liquor and was free in showing his money and nice firearms—one of which he sold to some of the whites or Indians who loaf around the ferry." [17]

William Henry Humphrey, "the Jack Screw," left the Bristol Train "at noon on his pony to go ahead & overtake some friends   Have travelled this afternoon about 12 miles making 20 today - very good considering we have ferried the Pont Newf ..."   Joe Sprott and Hank Ryerly "on guard tonight."[J]

Saturday, 9 August, Jane Gould, "This morning we saw Salmon River Mountains away off as far as we could see. We are in sight of Three Buttes, they are forty-four miles from the road."[G]

Five

Attacks Near Massacre Rocks

For many years a popular rest stop and camp area for travelers along the Oregon Trail was by a large rock upon which many emigrants inscribed their names. It is protected now and is known as Register Rock.[1]

Two miles to the East wagon trains passed through a narrow, high, lava rock defile, some 1,250 miles along the Oregon Trail from Independence, Missouri. This was a dramatic Oregon Trail site known as "Devil's Gate" and "Gate of Death" to the emigrants. Devil's Gate Pass lies between the rocky cliffs of a wild volcanic formation and is all that remains of an extinct volcano.[2] Interstate-86 uses the considerably widened "defile" now.

East of Massacre Rocks the Oregon Trail route went through a natural trap of steep grades descending and arising from a deep hazardous ravine that menaced wagon-train emigrants. This spot was recognized as the most dangerous point along the Oregon Trail in Idaho.[3]

In 1912 the name "Massacre Rocks" was applied to the area as a successful local promotional device. The granite monument placed in the defile in 1927 referred to the skirmishes between Shoshone Indians and emigrants beginning with attacks on two wagon trains. These encounters took place east of the pass and involved emigrant trains strung along the nine miles of trail to American Falls.[4]

On Saturday, 9 August 1862, five emigrant trains were traveling the Oregon Trail following the south side of the Snake River. Four passed by the Americans Falls and the other, the Walker-Wilson Ox Train, would pass there the next day.

The Iowa City Train was furthest west, nearest to the Massacre Rocks. Some three miles behind them came the Adams Train. Then four miles further back was the Kennedy Train and two miles more was the Bristol Train, the closest to American Falls.[5]

The Kennedy Train had camped on Snake river. That morning they traveled seven miles and reached the American Falls on the Snake River.[JM] Hamilton Scott noted that the Falls, "is one of the natural curiosities. The water falls forty or fifty feet over rocks and makes a great roaring noise."[HS]

Henry Judson recorded that the Bristol Train had got

an early start & soon reach the South bank of the Snake river - A pretty moderate clear stream from a half to three fourths of a mile wide & follow down on a bluff - so dusty at a distance we come unexpectedly upon the Falls which deserve more than a passing notice - Above the fall the river is about a half mile wide & narrows through hugh piles of volcanic rocks to a quarter of a mile - The whole fall is probably 30 ft but no one place exceeds 10 ft descent. The water tumbles promiscuously over rocks a perfect foam for an eighth of a mile & glides smoothly away - A huge rock near the middle divides the stream like Niagara & taken together the fall bows in the same way   Sheppard who has seen both says this is equal in beauty & grandeur to the falls of St. Anthony in Minnesota.[J]

Some of our boys were left behind ... near the falls to fish.[J]

Five year old Christina Taylor Chambers did not remember seeing any soldiers on the trail. None were near this day when their help was needed. This the Indians were well aware of.[6]

They were "in the very midst of a great danger and seemed to be almost entirely unconscious of it." About 5 p.m. John Hileman was "riding ahead of the train a mile or so in search of grass and a camping place at which we might remain over Sunday. On looking up the road ahead of me I saw a horseman coming towards me in a hasty manner ... This was a rare thing to see any person coming eastward."[H]

]   Attack on the Iowa City Train   [

The mule train that started out from Iowa City as the "Salmon River Party" had Andrew J. Hunter as its captain. It was identified as the "Iowa City Train" by other emigrants on the trail (and for some reason later called the "Smart Train.") Henry Judson recorded that "a mule train from Iowa City had first been attacked."[J] Alvin Zaring noted that the train first attacked was "of eleven wagons had sixty-five head of cattle and twelve head of horses"[7] and the Scott brothers, "a horse train of about 12 wagons."[HS RS]

Charles M. Harrison, a member of this train, wrote a letter three days following the attack, dated 11 August 1862, Raft River, Washington Territory:

Our train at the time of the attack consisted of eight wagons, having been joined by one wagon from Leavenworth and one from Minnesota; we had seventeen men, but five of them had stopped to fish, and were prevented by the Indians from joining us in time to render us any assistance.

We were passing through a very broken and rocky country, about twenty miles below the American Falls, on the Snake river, not for a moment harboring any suspicions of danger.[8]

They were actually some nine miles below the American Falls, about a half mile east of Massacre Rocks.[9] This Indian attack probably commenced well before mid-morning. Harrison:

our hindmost wagon, which was about three hundred yards in our rear, was suddenly attacked by some twelve or fourteen Indians. They came out of a ravine on the left of a road, and commenced the attack with bows and arrows, riding along side and shooting at the two men in the wagon, one of which was wounded in three places, but they still urged on their horses, until the Indians shot one of their animals, and by this means succeeded in stopping their team, and upsetting the wagon. The two men then left their team and ran up to us amid a perfect shower of arrows and bullets.

Mr. Hunter, who was Captain of our little train, gave orders to the men to get ready their firearms and prepare for fight, and right speedily was the order obeyed, considering the surprise in which we were taken, together with the fact that perhaps not one of us had ever been called upon to defend our lives or property by the use of such weapons. The Indians then began to circle round us, yelling and discharging their guns at random into our midst. They could not have chosen a better place to attack us, as there was a little ravine on either side of our wagons. After discharging several shots at us in this manner, some of them rode up one of the ravines and dismounting, crawled up through the sage brush—which was very thick—to within a short distance of us, and we had no indication of their whereabouts until we heard the sharp crack of a rifle and the death-dealing missile came whizzing through the air, striking Hunter in the neck. He sank to the ground, and spoke but a few words before he expired. The savage yell which rose from those pirates of the plains denoted their satisfaction in the deed, and again the bullets came whistling through the air, penetrating our wagons, or burying themselves with a dull thud in the ground around us.

We then moved to a position about fifty yards in advance, and a little to the left of the road, where the ground was higher and better calculated for defense. Soon after arriving at this point a bullet passed through the coat sleeve of A.J. Cassady, cutting through his shirt, but not touching his arm. A moment after, he fell, seriously, but not dangerously wounded by a ball in the hip. Matters looked doubtful about this time, and our position seemed very critical, but we kept up firing whenever we could see an Indian, although with little hopes of hitting them, for they rode like demons, turning their horses here and there, now sitting erect in their saddles, now throwing themselves flat along their horses' backs, or completely hiding themselves behind the bodies of their ponies. Whenever we shot, we would swing our hats and howl our defiance at them in a manner which seemed to scare them more than our bullets. They kept around us for about two hours, when they withdrew, carrying with them the plunder from the captured wagon, and driving off two mules. We then moved to a place of greater safety, about a quarter of a mile from the scene of action, and camped.[10]

The attack had lasted about two hours or more before the train moved on to a "place of greater safety." This would be at or near the Massacre Rocks defile. "Here we waited in a state of deep suspense for the return of our comrades, four of whom came safely into camp, but the body of the fifth ... was found by some of them lying in a ravine pierced through by a rifle ball."

In addition to Capt. Hunter the other man killed of the Iowa City Train was an Italian from St. Paul, Minnesota named Masemo Lepi (Massimo Lippi).[G]   While the Iowa City train waited for the men who had been fishing along the Snake River, another train was being attacked.

]   A Second Train Attacked   [

The horseman coming eastward along the road in a hasty manner that John Hileman saw while riding a mile or so ahead of the Bristol train was William Henry Humphrey.[H]   Hank Humphrey was the powerful man that Henry Judson called the "Jack Screw."[J] Hank had left the Bristol Train the day before to overtake a friend of his who he learned was in a train two days ahead.[H] He had caught up with the Kennedy train and stayed all night with them. Continuing on ahead he was riding along alone when he nearly ran on to the Indians—they were attacking a train.[J]

Some two miles beyond the American falls the Kennedy Train had stopped for dinner on the banks of a little brook and to let their stock graze.[JM]   Humphry rushed up on his pony and called out in excitement, "The Indians are robbing a train 4 miles ahead. Come quick."[RS]

Some of the men started immediately to give assistance to the train of thirteen wagons ahead.[11]   About 145 men grabbed their guns mounted horses and rushed ahead as fast as the horses could go.[RS] The rest of the Kennedy Train hitched up without finishing their dinner and drove on as fast as they could punch the ox teams along.[HS]

According to Bristol, "The only horse saved was rescued from an Indian by one of my train named Hank Humphrey ... An Indian mounting a large iron-gray horse belonging to the train" being attacked had "some difficulty in managing him, when Hank seized the horse and dismounted the Indian, who ran away. Hank vaulted upon his back and at full speed hastened to inform" the trains. Hank told the rest of the Kennedy train of what was going on as he flew past it.[B]

When attacked the Adams Train was five or six miles ahead of the Bristol Train. Hank Humphrey "hastened to inform our train, which he did in perhaps forty minutes."[B] The first thing he said to Hileman was, "My God, John, the Indians have massacred a train and robbed them of all they had and they are only a short distance from us."[H]

Hileman, ahead of his train, "at once became conscious of our extreme danger and turned back to inform the train and bring up the wagons which were lagging behind and I expected an attack to be made any moment. Learning that two ox teams were ahead of us and going to camp at or near the battlefield, we pushed on to overtake them."[H]

It was soon after 4 o'clock when Judson saw Humphrey returning to the Bristol train "on a strange horse in great haste to inform us that a party of 150 Indians have attacked a train ahead - have killed one man mortally wounded another & slightly wounded 3 men - driven off the stock & pillaged the train … He caught a horse which had broken away from them, left his pony & mounted him & hurried back, to hurry up to the scene The Newbern Colony & Capt Kenneddy trains."[J]

After coming on to the Bristol Train, Humphrey then went on to the next train three or four miles further in the rear and informed them of what was going on. This could be the Thompson train of 20 wagons.[12 J]

In ten minutes Bristol had his train moving forward with all possible speed. A company of sharp-shooters struck off to the left, to the south, to cut off the Indians retreat to the mountains. [B] In an hours driving the Bristol train came "to the place where the horrible scene took place."[H]

]   The Adams Train   [

"Whether or not the Indians planned to hit the second wagon train, we will never know. It is likely they came upon it on their way back to their camp." The mounted Shoshoni and Bannock of the area roamed freely and widely over the Snake River Plain. They were very much aware of what was happening around them, and news traveled fast.[13]

Hamilton Scott thought the thirteen wagons that had been attacked and taken by the Indian "was only a small train of eleven teams;" his brother, Scott, thought eighteen and Charles Harrison, an ox train of twelve wagons. But Charles Bullwinkle, from New York City was then traveling with Adams. There were only 25 men in the train and a few women.[HS 14]

The train was quietly wending its way on the road, but was very much scattered. Bullwinkle was nearly a mile in advance of the train in his light wagon.[15] He was the first one killed, "the Indians coming upon either side and killing him almost instantly."[B]

Without any previous warning, the others of the Adams train were attacked by seventy-five to one hundred mounted Indians. Others thought not less than 200 Indians made the attack.[HS] "They were, attacked in a narrow canyon where there were lots of big rocks to hide behind, big as-a house."[RS] Captain Adams tried to form a corral[J] but they could not form any sort of defense.

In an interview 65 years later, Margaret Stoot Thiel's recollection differed somewhat from other accounts. "When the party had been attacked the men had stacked the feather beds inside of the wagons and had the women lie down in the wagons while the men tried to fight off the Indians. The Indians, however, rode past the back of the wagons and shot at the women from the rear of the wagon. One of the young women climbed out of the wagon and, holding a heavy bread-board in front of her, tried to escape, but an Indian shot through the bread-board."[16]

It was Miss Elizabeth Adams, "a highly accomplished and beautiful young lady," who was assisting her mother to escape while Captain Adams stepped to his wagon to get his money. It was then that his daughter was shot in the shoulder and fell.[17]

"When the little band, finding that their only hope was in retreat, left their wagons," many fled into the sage brush and escaped.[B] Some ran behind the bluffs. Three men with good rifles got behind a bluff and fired until one was wounded. They then fled after having seen five Indians fall."[J]

"They killed one man and wounded another in the arm and seriously wounded a woman who was shot in the neck."[HS] So, one man killed and three wounded, and one woman. Lizzie Adams, severely wounded.[EM]

]   Kennedy Train Rescue   [

The men from the Kennedy train coming up to where the Adams train had been attacked drove the Indians away.[B] "But before arriving at the scene of action we met a woman who had been shot through the breast, and also a number of children, who were in a perfect state of frenzy."[18]

Robert Scott "met a lot of the emigrants coming to meet us, crying for help, big strong men and women, stood there crying like children. They had to run for their lives, were bareheaded. barefooted, with nothing left but what was on their backs, had to run and let the Indians take everything. We rushed on, but the Indians had taken everything but the wagons."[RS]

"They took all provisions, bedding and stock, all but the wagons and yokes and chains, emptied out feathers and straw beds."[RS] "They had gone leaving the empty and naked wagons even taking the covers off the wagons."[HS] "The ground was covered with feathers, flour, corn, etc."[J] Margaret Stoot Thiel recalled:

> The Indians ripped open the feather beds, throwing the feathers out on the prairie and taking the ticks. They also ripped open the sacks of flour, shook the flour out and took the flour sacks. When our wagon train came to where the other train had been attacked we tried to gather up some of the flour, also to gather up the feathers. In scooping up the feathers, one of the party came across a purse with over $800 in it. The owner had hidden the purse in the feather bed.[19]

The Indians got into some timber in the foothills out of sight. The Kennedy men "followed them a long way until about 4 o'clock. They knew we were after them so they scattered in the hills and timber. We only got 14 oxen." As the oxen could not travel very fast the Kennedy men were able to run up on them, and the Indians ran."[RS]

> We got the cattle back to where the wagons were, and our own train, had come up and was waiting for us. The Indians only killed one man, Mr. Bullwinkel from New York, but wounded Several men and one woman. We took these people in with us, tied their wagons behind ours and hauled them 4 or 5 miles and camped. We will divide up so they can get along and take them on through, give women and men clothing and food and put oxen on their wagons to get along. We could do nothing else and be human, and they were very thankful for help.[RS]

"One of the party, named Bullwinkle, from New York city, was killed and robbed of between six and seven thousand dollars."[20] Henry Judson "saw one of Mr. Bullwinke's cards on which beside his name was 374 Sixth Avenue New York." His four horses and $6000 in money was taken.[J]

Also Judson was "inclined to the belief that Bulwinkels gold tempted the cupidity of the men at Port-Newf ferry & that they came to the Indian village & by promises of plunder easily persuaded them to undertake the Capture of the weak & almost defenseless party - The white men probably took the gold & let the Indians pillage for their share."[J]

It was reported that at the Portneuf ferry "Charles Bullwinkle had taken a little liquor and was free in showing his money and nice firearms—one of which he sold to some of the whites or Indians who loaf around the ferry ... while Bullwinkle was nearly a mile in advance of the train, he was shot dead by the identical gun no doubt, which he had sold."[21]   Jane Gould had heard that Bullwinkle

> was shot eight times, his dog was shot four times before he would let them get to the wagon. They took all that he had in the wagon except his trunks and books and papers. They broke open his trunks and took all that they contained (he had six) it is supposed that they took six thousand dollars from him, tore the cover from his wagon, it was oil cloth. He had four choice horse, they ran away when he was shot. The harnesses were found on the trail where it was cut from them as they went, it was a nice silver mounted one.[G]

Where Adams Train was Attacked

Looking West. Snake River on the right.

Photo by Author, 16 June 2007.

SIX

Encampment at Massacre Rocks

The Newbern-Kennedy Train continued on the trail hauling the Adams Train wagons to a suitable camping place about four miles down the trail.[HS] They traveled only two miles further when they found a wagon that had been upset and partly robbed.[JM] There was a dead man lying near. They traveled half a mile farther and overtook the first train that had been attacked.[JM] "Here we found a horse train of about 12 wagons that was attacked at about the same time that the other train was. Eight of their horses were stolen and 2 of their men killed."[HS 1]

When the Kennedy Train "went into camp there were 12 wagons in another train came to us and asked to stay with our train until we all got through. They had been attacked today at another place and lost 8 horses and two men were killed by Indians. They had a hard fight, but saved most of their outfit, but were badly scared and did not want to travel alone any more."[RS]

Toward night the Iowa City Train was joined by the two large trains. Charles Harrison and the others "rejoiced that we were once more in comparative safety."

Some of our men also brought us the sad intelligence that an ox train of twelve wagons had been taken by the Indians three miles back, who took everything in the train, leaving the families that composed it entirely destitute. In this train there was one man killed, one woman, it is feared, fatally wounded, and several men slightly.[2]

The three trains camping together that night formed a corral of eighty-six wagons. That night they prepared for burial of the dead.[3]

]   Bristol Train   [

After being warned by Hank Humphrey of the Indian attack on the Adams Train, the Bristol Train drove on for an hour. They "came to the place where the horrible scene took place, but found the Indians had run off the stock, taking provisions, clothing, etc. of the train, but left the wagons which the ox trains ahead of us had taken and gone in pursuit of grass."[H]

Hileman "found quite a quantity of blood and fragments of such things as emigrants usually carry with them, and it was evident that the Indians had done their hellish deeds in a hasty manner and left. The place selected by them for the attack was the best on the road and not far distant from the road which turns down to Salt Lake, which I learned is 175 miles south of us."[H]

Humphrey returned to the Bristol Train and reported having seen the Indians going over the hills driving the stock they had taken from the attacks.[J]   When the Bristol men "struck the Indians' trail they had passed and were beyond our reach."[B]

The Bristol Train pushed on endeavoring to catch the Kennedy-Adams Trains which had gone ahead to find grass. They drove very late until after sundown.

The Bristol men, who had been on the Indians' trail, got back to the road where the attack was made. Their "animals were so tired we could not proceed and had to stop right there, though there was little forage."[B] It was about a mile from the scene of the attack and they had "only got a short distance on account of the darkness ... with the blood of innocent men and women. We at once put out a strong picket guard on the surrounding hills, got a hasty supper in the dark, staked out mules in the sage brush and hoped the night would be a hasty one."[H]

Soon Thompson's ox train of twenty wagons came up "making us pretty strong." The emigrants expected an attack that night. Bristol "put the camp in order, and, with Ives, our famous hunter, stationed ourselves in a nest of rocks which commanded the ravine down which they were expected to come. We thought it quite likely we should be killed, but hoped so to demoralize them by vigorous defense of our castle as to save our train."[B]

"Our two trains put out a strong picket guard of which" Judson served "on the last watch ... All quiet though we believe we are watched." But the long night passed, and no attack.[B]

]   Emigrants Gather   [

The next morning was the Sabbath, 10 August. By four o'clock, daybreak, the Bristol Train pushed on as they needed to get to grass for the ox teams. After traveling about three miles, they reached the place where they "learned that a mule train from Iowa City had first been attacked, nearly at the same time the attack on the ox train of thirteen wagons." A little further they find the Newbern-Kennedy Train and "the wrecks of the mule train of 11 wagons & the Ox trains all together."[J]

For once on the Sabbath the Bristol Train "hitched up and drove forward five miles to where there was grass and water, and where lay our dead and wounded fellow-travelers. We at once undertook our share of the work burying the dead, caring for the wounded, providing places for the fugitives in the trains, and furnishing them with provisions and clothing."[B]

As they went into camp for the day with the ox trains close by them, those of the Bristol Train learned that in addition to Mr. Adams being murdered the day before, "two men from the mule train were found dead beside the road. One a Mr. Hunter of Iowa City & the other an Italian." Judson stated, "It is believed these depredations are instigated & led by Morman men with white blood in their veins."[J]

A news article from Carson City, and reprinted in Sacramento and San Francisco, contained information about the attacks given by arriving emigrants of what they had heard, so sensational and speculative.

> They know that white men were concerned in the massacre, for some 15 were seen lying on a high bench of land beckoning and directing the Indians ... their stock, wagons, clothing, food, and the valuable lives, taken by the fiends in human shape, who appear to infest that part of the route for no other purpose than to murder and rob for a livelihood. An Indian afterward told some of them he "heap like whites; he live with um white man's wife." No doubt referring to the kind of people what were helping on these massacres.[4]

It could well be so that the attacks were "instigated" by white men or men of white and Indian parentage. White men, so-called "White Indians" or "renegades," were involved in the July 1859 attack on the Shepherd Train on the Hudspeth Cutoff. Although painted to look like Indians, they were identified as white by a woman they ravaged as they had not bothered to paint all parts of their bodies. A month later, in August 1859 just east of the American Falls, a survivor of the Miltimore massacre identified those who initiated the attack as men painted to look like Indians who spoke English quite well and acted accordingly. Some of these men may have had ties to the Mormon community for trading purposes. But if they claimed to be LDS, they were not good Mormons.[*]

From the encampment a party was sent out to gather what was left of any value of the Adams Train. "Everything that was worth taking apparently had been tied on the oxen by the robbers, and the balance—flour, feather beds, etc.—destroyed … A stock of a silver-mounted gun, which belonged to Bullwinkle, was found among some rocks, and was taken to camp where it was put up at auction and bid off at $43. The money, with provisions and clothing, was handed over to the destitute survivors, most of whom came on with Capt. Wood's train."[5]

"Our camp is a sorry one today - scarcely a smile to be seen & the jokes are infrequent." Captain Kennedy sold, at auction, "the effects of the dead to supply the pressing wants of the poor wretches who have been robbed - A fine lot of books are sold & among them I noticed an Unabridged Webster's Dictionary brought $3.00. Hank bought a little paper" which enabled Judson "to continue this narrative."[J]

During the forenoon, about nine o'clock, the remains of the men were laid in their graves:[J] Charles Bullwinkle, Andrew J. Hunter, and Masemo Lepi.[G]

Harrison: "The body of Mr. Hunter was followed to the grave with deep sorrow, not only by those who had long known his many virtues and endearing qualities of head and heart, but also by many who had met him on the plains for the first time,

---

[*]The Mormons, LDS, have become most patriotic of Americans. See Volume I, *The Boise Massacre on the Oregon Trail*, Chapters 16 and 17 for 1859 attacks on emigrant trains.

and had already marked him as a man of unwavering integrity and honor.* We laid him to rest by the roadside, by the banks of the Snake river."[6]

The three dead were buried but the affair did not end there.[H]

---

*Years later, in the midst of winter, Captain Andrew Hunter's brother, Joseph, was found dead by the side of the Oregon Short Line railroad track three miles east of Caldwell, Idaho. Joseph Hunter was a pioneer of that place. Among his belongings was a clipping titled, "Early Day Indian Fight," from the Idaho City *Idaho World*, dated 31 March 1911. It was an account of the killing of Andrew J. Hunter.

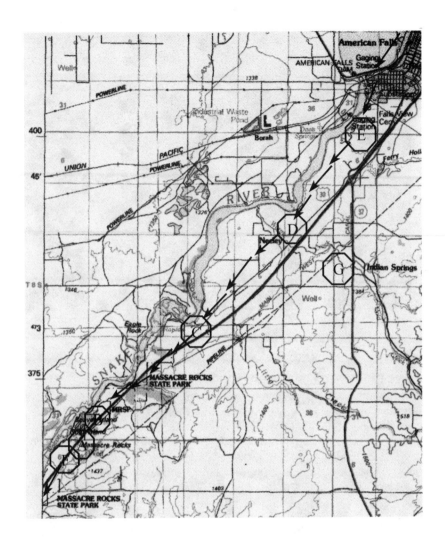

Massacre Rocks Encounters, 9–10 August 1862

A. Devil's Gate Pass. **B**. Attack on Iowa City Train. **C**. Attack on Adams Train. **D**. Kennedy Train. **E**. Bristol Train. **F**. Emigrant Gathering. **G**. Skirmish with Indians toward Indian Springs.

Pocatello ID 1:100,000 scale topographic map. Scale: vertical grid lines = 5,280 feet or 1 statue mile. Arrows indicate Oregon Trail.

(Compiled by Author.)

Massacre Rocks Defile

Top: Looking southwest from Visitor's Center, across I-86. Monument is at the base of the rock on the right.

Bottom: Looking northeast from the I-86 overpass. This is where the emigrants gathered following attacks in August 1862.

Photos by Author, 2 April 2008

SEVEN

Pursuit of the Indians

About noon on this Sunday, 10 August 1862, several of the horses of the robbed Adams Train were "artfully led out upon a hillside in full view and appeared to be loose and feeding at leisure." Captain Kennedy came to the Bristol Train and proposed they should go out and drive them in. Bristol objected, "saying it was a ruse of the Indians to get us out there to shoot us from their ambuscades. That each horse, no doubt, had a lasso attached to his foot, and an Indian was crawling after him and when we came nigh would shoot us, then mount and run away. But Captain Kennedy would go, and told others Bristol was a coward."[B]

William Redhoffer thought that Captain Kennedy "acted an honorable part, and proved himself worthy of the gratitude which was exhibited by the emigrants on the occasion."[1]

Captain Kennedy raised a company of 35–40 well armed and mounted men and led them out to attempt to recover the stolen stock and property from the Indians.[2] Henry Judson: the stock of the wagon trains were closely watched while about 35 armed men started back to the scene of the murders to reconnoiter.[J]

Of the several accounts recorded of the skirmish, only Robert C. Scott's diary of 12 January 1863 indicated that he might have been with the party:

Captain Kennedy with 35 men went out to try and get the 8 horses back. Out about 9 miles in the hills the Indians were guarding the horses in a canyon. When they saw us they began riding around the stock stolen, in a circle and shooting arrows under the horses neck, hanging on the opposite side from us. There were about 75 to 100 Indians. We stood our ground and after we had dropped about 20 Indians they became scattered and in 20 minutes more they all were out in every direction and gone. We surrounded the horses and brought them in to camp. We lost two of our men in the fight. Thos. Newman from our train and one man from the other train, don't know his name, were killed by the Indians. These men got away from the rest of us and were killed. Capt. Kennedy was shot through the side and Mr. Taylor through the leg and several others got slight wounds.[RS]

Hamilton Scott recorded a differing account. "When about 9 miles from Camp a band of Indians came on their horses meeting" the armed emigrants.

The Indians at once raised a white flag. One of the boys shot at them. The Indians immediately raised a war-whoop and began circling our boys. They fought them for about 3 miles killing 2 of our company and wounding several others. Capt Kennedy mortally wounded, shot through the side just above the hip bone. Tom Newman and one other missing, supposed to be killed. There is now 4 or 5 trains camped here.[HS]

The volunteers came upon the Indians just south of the Indian Springs Natatorium location.[3] This would be about seven miles northeast of the emigrants encamped near the

Massacre Rocks defile and less than two miles southeast of the Oregon Trail. In John Hileman's letter, written the next day:

> Some 30 men from the 2 ox teams and the trains attacked the previous day, started out in pursuit of the Indians and their stock. After travelling some 7 miles in the direction in which the Indians went they came suddenly upon them and a fight immediately commenced. At first fire 3/4 of the white men ran and the red men pursued, and after a running fight of some 3 miles, the Indians ceased pursuit.[H]

Louisa Paul: "So our Captain thought he would make up a company and go out and whip the Indians and get back some of the stock in order to help these poor people to their destination. The Indians were too many for them and drove the Captain and his men back upon the Snake river. As they came into sight of the river, another train of wagons was coming, so the Indians then left them."[4] It was the arrival of the Walker Train.

Jane Gould heard that the Indian chief appeared "in a suit of Mr. Bullwinkel's." Some of the Indians on ponies that surrounded the Kennedy force had the best kind of rifles, some of which shot Minnie balls.[G]

Kennedy's force "were repulsed with a loss of four killed and fourteen wounded." Another account reported that "Capt K. killed nine Indians. Of the volunteers four men were killed and seven wounded."[5]

]   Search for the Dead   [

Four men, who were going east, had arrived in camp with their pack animals. They were just from the Salmon River and Powder River mining areas. Henry Judson and others in the

Bristol Train had invited one of the packers, L. Billman of Iowa, to dinner. Just as they sat down an express rider came for the Doctor to attend Captain Kennedy. The express rider reported that about five miles back from the road the Kennedy force came upon 20 Indians with the stock. The Indians were armed with rifles, which carry 200 yards. At the first firing a part of the volunteers stampeded. Kennedy, in trying to rally the men, was badly wounded. The party fell back to the road where there was an Ox train of 10–12 wagons passing. When the express rider left, the party was trying to keep the Indians at bay.[J]

Their dinner table was immediately deserted. Joe Hileman, Hank Humphrey, with the dinner guest, Billman, joined a party to go to the assistance of the volunteers. They left immediately. Captain Bristol with a few more soon followed, making a reinforcement of 30–35 men.[J]

Those in the camp were on the alert and brought the stock close in. Speculation ran high as to the number and intention of the Indians. "All are agreed that they are led by a good proportion of white men - perhaps renegades & perhaps not from Salt Lake - Some think they have recognized men seen at the ferry of the Pont-Newf."[J] Hileman wrote, "After we learned of the fate of the last party the greatest excitement prevailed in camp and a small party went to their assistance to recover the dead and wounded."[H]

Captain Bristol remembered that in an hour or two Kennedy "sent to me saying he had fallen into an ambush, was badly wounded, and wished me to come to his rescue." He did so, but the Indians "fled at our approach. Captain Kennedy was brought off, but two of his men were left dead in the sage brush." We "tried to find them but could not."[B]

Joe Sprott and Henry Humphrey with 14 others went far out among the hills to look for the dead and wounded.[J] One of the men "was not found and one had been scalped, the first scalped man" Hileman had seen. The Indians that he alluded to in his letter "were Snakes, and it is thought were in large force."[H]

The fight as learned by Henry Judson "was a very serious affair. The party of the morning were 7 or 8 miles from the road when they discovered the Indians & then began a running fight for that distance ... Six Indians and some ponies were known to be killed." Four of Captain Kennedy's force "are killed & 3 wounded himself among the latter & tis feared mortally ... Two of his men who were killed were left among the Indians from necessity ... One of the killed was scalped."[J]

Jane Gould heard, "One of those killed was Capt. Adams' son, the other was a young man in the Kennedy train."[G] George W. Adams' sons were involved in the pursuit of the Indians. The day before, his daughter, Elizabeth, was the woman who was so badly wounded. Now, his son, George W., age 24 was killed.[EM] Another son, a young lad, Thomas J. Adams, was wounded in the fracas. "He is a brave boy & tis known he killed an Indian." Their "grandfather was killed by Indians in Kentucky."[J]

Henry Judson listed the names of the men killed as "C. Leeker [G. Leeper] & Geo. Adams ... the missing & believed to be killed are Noonan [Newman] & Wm. Motes ... All of Iowa ... The Italians name was Massimo Lippi."[J] Judson misidentified George Leeper and Thomas Newman. John Hileman listed the six killed in the attacks on the trains and the pursuit of the Indians as "A.J. Winter, Iowa City; Masemo Lepi, St. Paul Minn.; Chas. Bulwinkle, New York City; George Sheperi, Iowa City; George W. Adams, Iowa City; Italian, name unknown." He misidentified Andrew J. Hunter as "A.J. Winter" and Leeper as "Sheperi."[H]

The two men who were missing, and supposed killed, were Thomas Newman of the Kennedy Train and William Motes.[HS]
[H] Hamilton Scott: "Newman was seen to fall in the battle."[HS] Robert Scott:

7 of our men have died, making a total of 9 men the past two weeks from Indians fights and thousands of dollars in stock and supplies. We never can know how many Indians were killed, but we are sure their number was many more, two of our men we never got, the Indians carried them away. We saw them fall in the battle, But thought best not to follow for them as the Indians had the advantage of knowing the country and where to hide and take advantage of us, so we returned to our train to protect our own.[RS]

]   The Encamped Emigrants   [

On that Sunday, 10 August, Jane Gould in the Wilson Train that had joined the Walker Train:

Traveled five or six miles when we came to Snake River, followed it up two or three miles where we came to the American Falls, it is quite a sight, it falls over rocks, there are two or three little rock islands in it which makes it a second Niagra. We nooned there so had time to examine it closely, some of the men caught some very nice trout. We staid till two o'clock then traveled till about four or five when we from the back of the train saw those on ahead all get out their guns. In a short time the word came back that a train six miles on had been attacked by the Indians and some killed and that was cause enough for the arming, in short time we were met by two men … We learned that a train of eleven wagons had been plundered of all that was in them and the teams taken and three men killed. One was Mr. Bullwinkle who left us on the 25th of last month at the crossing of Green River, he went on with this Adams train, was intending to wait for us but we had not overtaken him yet.[G]

The two men wanted men from the Wilson Train "to go a short distance from the road and bring up two dead men to this camp five miles ahead. Albert unloaded his little wagon and sent Gus back with them and about forty armed men from both trains to get them."[G]

Robert Scott pointed out that Capt Kennedy and Ephraim Taylor had to be carried "on stretchers, because they could not stand the jolt of the wagons. Men took turns carrying."[RS] Jane Gould:

Those that were carried to camp were those killed this morning. Mr. Bullwinkel and the two others were buried before we got to the camp. There were one hundred and fifty wagons there and thirty-four of ours. Capt. Kennedy was severely wounded. Capt. Hunter of the Iowa City Train was killed likewise an Italian. We camped near Snake River. We could not get George to ride after the news, he would walk and carry his loaded pistol, if there was any shooting going on he wanted to help. (George 10 years old was son of the author- the pistol was a muzzle-loading affair).[G]

Late in the evening both parties returned along with Captain Walker's train and the smaller Wilson Train that Judson had mentioned. "They have had a hard time & are nearly tired out - The wailings of the friends of the killed & wounded can be heard throughout the camp & are truly heart rending - One of the killed was scalped."[J] When Bristol returned he "found we had twenty-one on hand, killed or wounded" from the two days of encounters.

Two of them were women. How hard it was for me to persuade the wives of the men left in the field not to insist on our going back to recover their bodies, as in that case we should probably lose more men. Captain

Kennedy's wound was at first considered mortal, as it struck him in the abdomen and came out behind, near the backbone, and was supposed to have passed through the intestines.[B]

H.F. Swasley must have been one of those returning: "On arriving at camp we found that Captain John Walker's train of forty-six wagons had come in during our absence; a double guard was posted, the fires put out, and the band of emigrants spent the night in administering such remedies for the wounded as were at hand."[6]

Just at dark "Capt Dan's Co which we left at Green River ferry came up" and Henry Judson estimated "a tent city of probably 600 souls."[J] According to John Hileman "2 more ox teams came into camp making now some 200 wagons and 400 men and 300 women and children."[H]

This day, Sunday, "A couple in Capt K's train were to have been married ... but postponed the ceremony indefinitely." Judson continued, "Some of our boys were left behind yesterday near the falls to fish & came late to camp & knew nothing of the disturbance till they reached camp - They caught a fine mess of fish & among them a nice trout or two."[J]

Casualties near Massacre Rocks
9–10 August 1862

Killed in Encounters Near Massacre Rocks–8

9 August
† Andrew J. Hunter   Captain of Iowa City Train
† Massimo O. Lippi* (Masemo Lepi, Luper)   Iowa City Train
† Charles Bullwinkle (Bullwinkel)   Adams Train

10 August
† George W. Adams, age 24   Adams Train
† George Leeper (Sheperd, Sheperi, Liffe), 20   Adams Train
Thomas Newman (Noonan)   missing & supposed killed
William Motes   missing & supposed killed

11 August
Miss Elizabeth J. Adams died, age 26   Adams Train

Wounded in Encounters Near Massacre Rocks–11

Thomas J. Adams	Jonathan (John) Miller
Giovanni Benvenuti (Bennetti)	John Patterson
Thomas Bradford	E. A. (P. O.) Sullivan
A. J. Cassady	Ephraim Taylor
Jason Crawford	John Walker
John K. Kennedy	

*Masemo Lipi was fishing, killed, found in a ravine.
†5 Buried at Massacre Rocks.

Casualties near Massacre Rocks.   (Compiled by Author.)

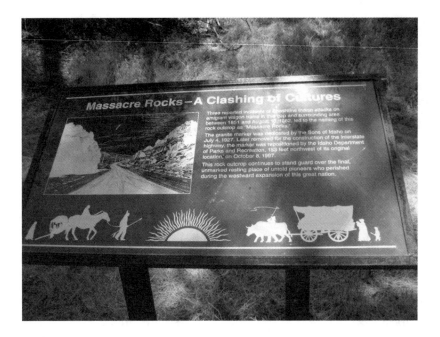

Massacre Rocks—A Clashing of Cultures

Three reported incidents of Shoshone Indian attacks on emigrant wagon trains in this gap and surrounding area between 1851 and August 10, 1862, led to the naming of this rock outcrop as "Massacre Rocks."

The granite marker was dedicated by the Sons of Idaho on July 4, 1927. Later removed for the construction of the Interstate highway, the marker was repositioned by the Idaho Department of Parks and Recreation, 153 feet northwest of its original location, on October 8, 1997.

This rock outcrop continues to stand guard over the final, unmarked resting place of untold pioneers who perished during the westward expansion of this great nation.

Reader Board, above, and monument located just on the north side of I-86 where the freeway passes through the Massacre Rocks defile. A path leads to the Massacre Rocks State Park Visitors Center.

MASSACRE ROCKS
ON
OLD OREGON TRAIL

IN THIS DEFILE ON AUGUST 10, 1862 A BAND OF SHOSHONE
INDIANS AMBUSHED AN IMMIGRANT TRAIN BOUND FOR OREGON
KILLING NINE WHITE MEN AND WOUNDING SIX.

————

ERECTED BY SONS OF IDAHO
1927

Elizabeth Adams Grave—Raft River.

Looking West to where Oregon & California Trail exit Raft River. On the right are the graves of Elizabeth Adams, Lydia Edmundson, and G. W. Sanders, behind a wood, rail fence. *Photo by Author, 11 August 1997.*

Raft River Trail Exit

Looking East across valley. OCTA members ~~wagons~~ vehicles circled around graves, where wagon trains camped. *Photo by Author, 11 August 1997.*

EIGHT

Raft River

Early in the morning of Monday, 11 August, the two men killed in pursuing the Indians, that were brought up by the Wilson Train, were buried with the other three killed on the 9th. George Adams and George Leeper made five men laid "side by side in this vast wilderness, killed by the guns and arrows of the red demons," according to Jane Gould.[G] H.F. Swasley indicated that "beneath the shadow of the inhospitable Snake river mountains, we laid them down in their final resting place."[1]

Robert Scott in the Kennedy Train estimated "the property and money the Indians stole from the train of 12 wagons and from the train we took in with us to be $11,000.00 all together, besides killing two of our men, whom we never recovered and our wounded may die."[RS] Judson wrote that "An effort is made to start a mounted party of 100 men to recover the bodies of the 2 missing men but Capt K's advice strongly urged is taken & the idea is abandoned."[J] Hamilton Scott: "We think it is not safe to go back to hunt the other 2 men for fear we lose more."[HS]

Robert Scott wrote: "Capt. Kennedy very bad condition from being shot. We are afraid he may not live, our doctor is alarmed about him."[RS] The news in the train Judson was in was that Kennedy "is reported better & some hopes are entertained of his recovery."[J] And Bristol: "Captain Kennedy's wound was at first considered mortal, as it struck him in the abdomen and came out behind, near the backbone, and was supposed to have passed through the intestines. It afterward proved to have gone around in the muscles."[B]

The Iowa City Mule Train of some eleven wagons concluded to travel with the Bristol Train. All the Captains decided to go on with their trains the thirteen miles to Raft river.[J] Sherlock Bristol stated that for various reasons the Kennedy Train "had lost all confidence in their officers, and, on the other hand, had unwarranted confidence in our train. They proposed to disband and join us. I objected, as it would make a body too unwieldy. At their earnest request we agreed to keep near them in our travel and camp by them for a time." Bristol surmised that this came from his going miles ahead of his train each afternoon to find a good campsite.[B]

"This morning we all started together after burying the dead."[H] "We did not get started till late."[G] "Twas a fine sight when all rolled out on to the road," about 9 o'clock "considerably over 200 wagons & mostly with long Ox teams & making a continuous train near or quite 3 miles long."[J]

James McClung: "We all hitched up and rolled out. Their was something over 200 wagons, Kenneday's train in the lead. Traveled 2 miles and crossed Fall Creek, traveled up a cannion near a half mile and struck high rolling ground and the roads were dusty. To wards night we camped on Raft River ... having traveled 13 miles."[JM]

Jane Gould said they "traveled twelve miles without stopping at noon, came up several steep hills, over one creek with three little falls, one above the other."[G] Henry Judson disagreed with McClung about which train was in the lead.

About 2 miles from Camp our train leading we come to
a pretty stream with a succession of small falls varying
from 2 ft to 6 or 8 in height between the place where

we ford it & its mouth - 3 miles farther we enter an ugly looking Canon of about a mile in length though a good road - Our Capt with his gun takes the top of the bluff on one side & Hollingshead the other & so we go through - Keeping a sharp eye out for Indians - We are not molested & soon after one oclk we reach Raft river a horridly crooked little narrow stream & camp on its west bank - many of us have walked the whole 13 miles & carried guns & I have not been so tired on the trip as today.

After about an hour & a half the Ox trains begin to come in & bedlam has begun - drivers yelling at their teams - children crowing & hallooring - cattle bellowing etc. all combine to make up a deafening hubbub & till all are finally settled in their respective Corralls confusion reigns supreme ... John writes home.[J]

John Hileman "came 13 miles to Raft River where we all camped for the day, and where I am writing this" letter.[H] He was not the only one to write as Charles M. Harrison wrote a letter to the *Iowa City State Press*, dating his letter "Raft River, Washington Territory, August 11, 1862."

Thinking that, perhaps, some tidings of the Iowa City "Salmon River party," would be of interest to some of your readers, have ventured to write you a brief communication, and in doing so it becomes my painful duty to send you the sad intelligence, (which will bring sorrow to the heart of many of your readers) of the death of Andrew J. Hunter, who was shot by the Snake Indians, in an engagement we had with them, on Saturday last, Aug. 9th, the circumstances of which I will briefly relate.

... The wounded are all doing well.

We apprehend no further danger as we will now travel with over one hundred teams ... Yours in great haste ... Chas. M. Harrison

In a private note accompanying the above letter, Mr. Harrison states that the party was getting along well since the fight with the Snakes. Cassaday's wound was not as painful as anticipated. The woman, however, mentioned as having been wounded on the ox train, did not survive her injuries.[2]

Hileman ended his letter, "Here the road forks, one for Oregon and Washington, and the other for California."[H]

]   Elizabeth Adams   [

The wounded daughter of Captain George Adams, died the evening of 11 August. She was buried the next morning beside another grave near Raft River. This brought the total number of emigrants killed near Massacre Rocks on 9–10 August to eight. H.F. Swasley:

On Tuesday morning, Miss Elizabeth Adams, a highly accomplished and beautiful young lady ... was buried amid the sobs of strong hearted men, and the quivering lips and moistened eyes of the company, showed that she had endeared herself to all by her gentleness and self-sacrificing bravery. The place where the company was camped was at the junction of the Oregon with the main California road and here Kennedy's Train left us, taking the Oregon road. Captain Kennedy and one of his men undoubted died afterward, as they were very severely wounded.[3]

Jane Gould also recorded that Captain Adams' daughter died "from the effects of her wound, was buried in a box made of a wagon box. Poor father and mother lost one son and one daughter, all of his teams, clothing, and four thousand dollars, is left dependent on the bounty of strangers ... Mrs. Ellen Jones (?) one of the ladies of the plundered train, her husband goes in the wagon just ahead of us. She was married the morning that she started for Cal. Not a very pleasant wedding tour."[G]

"Quite a subscription was raised in our camp this am for the relief of the robbed in the two small trains - Clothes & provisions of considerable amount were given & all," Henry Judson thought, that made them comfortable for the remainder of their journey.[J] The Scott brothers remarked that here some of their Kennedy Train "and the other train will leave us and take the road to California. We kept the old wagon road bearing northwest."[RS] Jane Gould noted there were two trains going to California that had started for Oregon.[G] Henry Judson on 12 August:

> We this morning bid good bye to Manning Mellus - Parkes - Lockwood - John Jones - Roberts - Owens Smith - Dr. Jones - Dickey & Westfall - They take the Cal road up Raft river bound for Southern Oregon while we keep our eyes straight ahead - No tears are shed & no regrets expressed - In fact we feel considerably relieved & think we have had our train purged of many a contrary - stubborn disposition & shall have less contention & fault finding - The above refers to only a part mentioned - We roll out with the Iowa City Train attached to ours making us still one team more then before they joined us & the above mentioned party left - As soon as Kenneddy's party bury the young woman Miss Elizabeth Adams who died last night they follow us close in our wake all day ... A

rumor we had in camp this morning of a train of 18 wagons being attacked on the road we have today driven over has we think proved a humbug … Capt K is reported to have stood the ride very well.[J]

Five days later, on 17 August, Evans S. McComas and his wagon trained crossed Raft River and continued west on the Oregon Trail. He observed the two graves in passing. The night before they had camped west of Massacre Rocks.

Last night our cattle got scared at a dog. We thought that the Indians had come to try us around. Every man was out with his gun in double quick. Traveled this forenoon 10 miles and crossed Raft Creek. From here we have to make 18 miles without water or grass. Lay by till 3 o'clock and then started over the sage plain. Roads very rock. Came 6 miles and encamped. Put the cattle in the corrall without water or grass. Found here the grave of G. W. Sanders, of Keokuk, Iowa, died July 27th. He had his horses stolen at Green river by Indians & stayed and hunted for them & exposure & trouble threw this man into a feaver from which he died. Also found the grave of Miss. E. I. Adams. Killed by Indians Aug. 9th, 62, age 26 years. Here the Smith Weston Train had been attacked by Indians. They killed 4 Indians and wounded 8 more without getting any of the men very much hurt. This road seems to be continual battle ground.[EM]

]   Pocatello's Northern Shoshoni   [

The land of the Northern Shoshoni band led by Pocatello (born 1815, died 1884) was an "expanse of country from upper

Goose Creek and an upper Humboldt-Thousand Springs area to Raft River, with City of Rocks a central feature in their territory. More possessive than many other Northern Shoshoni, they tended to exclude anyone else from utilizing that region." At times they were referred to as "wild wheat eaters." These people also harvested pine nuts around the City of Rocks area. That crop was isolated from other pine nut areas farther to the south, which gave Pocatello's band a distinctive culture. This Northern Shoshoni band also went northwest to fish at Salmon Falls on the Snake River. Sometimes they would go east to the Wind River and spend the winter with Chief Washakie's Eastern Shoshoni.[4]

In 1859 F.H. Lander was Superintendent of the *Fort Kearney, South Pass, and Honey Lake Wagon Road.* The expedition reached South Pass in June. As part of the official report, the Engineer of the Expedition, William H. Wagner, described his "intercourse with the Indians while in charge of the advance party."[5]

After the expedition left South Pass they "saw only a few lodges of Eastern Sho-sho-nees encamped on Green river. The main body of that tribe were on the eastern slope of the Wind River mountains. Passing from Green river we met none until we reached Soda Springs, where a single Indian came into our camp to trade some beaver skins. He belonged to the Sheepeaters tribe from the head-waters of Lewis Fork, and disclaimed any connection with the Bannocks. He informed me of the departure of the Bannocks for the mountains north of Snake river. It appears that they were afraid of the retaliations of traders or United States soldiers for their depredations committed on Green river and its vicinity last winter."

Lander's advance party left the Oregon Trail at the Snake River and followed the California Trail. When they reached the head of Raft creek, near City of Rocks, they met "Pocotaroh and a party of his band amounting to 15 warriors." Pocatello was expecting the Expedition as he "remembered the conditional promise given by" Lander the previous fall to return and bring presents.

Wagner observed that: "These Indians appeared destitute, almost, of the necessaries of life, and received with the greatest joy the presents" Lander had directed "to distribute among them. They were given blankets, cloth, handkerchiefs, knives, paints, and many other trifles, to which I added some flour."

Descending to Goose creek the advance party met several men of the Northern Shoshoni band "under the chief Ne-met-the. They were hunting in the Goose Creek mountains. I tried to engage one of them as guide, but the presence of some companies of the United States army, under the command of Major Lynde, intimidated them so much that they left again for the mountains." These soldiers were from Camp Floyd on Utah Lake. The advance party saw several bands of Weber River Indians in the upper part of Thousand Spring Valley who were also intimidated by the presence of soldiers.

On Hot Spring creek about 45 warriors came into the camp; inquired our intentions and those of the soldiers; avowed their honesty; that they had never stolen cattle or robbed emigrants. They received presents and departed without further molesting us, although only 6 persons were in camp at the time, the other members of my party being out on reconnoissance. On the upper part of Humboldt river several lodges were encamped. We saw, nightly, their campfires 3 or 4 miles from the road at the foot of the mountains. Many of them came into our camp begging and went away fully satisfied with the presents bestowed upon them.[6]

The soldier's had a camp on the north fork of Humboldt River. When the Lander advance party arrived there, Major Lynde had just returned from Gravelly Ford. Later, in his report, Wagner noted the "good conduct of Isaac Frapp, or Sho-sho-nee Aleck, the Sho-sho-nee half-breed, who has been of great service to the party, both as interpreter and as doing the general work of an employé." Lynde requested Alek Frapp to gather the Indians of the area. "Major Lynde made an appropriate speech, and presented" the Indians with flour and meat. The Indians informed Lynde that "most of their tribe had left the Humboldt and gone south to avoid the passing soldiers."

The advance party's reconnaissance sometimes extended 70 miles north of the Humboldt. They "met only a few lodges of Indians, belonging partly to the Sho-sho-nee and partly to the Bannock tribes. The latter came from the Snake river, where they had passed the fishing season. As they had never seen white men in this part of the country they were at a loss what to make of us, but, as I had always some presents with me, they seemed satisfied with the answer that we were here to see the country."

Wagner summarized that "All the Western Sho-sho-nees have been friendly to us, at least they did not molest us nor attempt to steal our mules. Close to the dividing range between the Western Sho-sho-nees and Pah-Utah tribes, we met about a dozen lodges of the latter Indians." These were the Northern Paiutes, who "received presents, but as their language is quite different from that of the Sho-sho nees, I was unable to learn any thing concerning them. These were the last party of Indians we saw, although delayed for some time in camp at Tutt's Meadows, Humboldt river."[7]

For two decades emigrant wagon traffic had traveled along the Snake River, up Raft River, through the City of Rocks and Granite Pass, Upper Goose Creek, and the headwaters of the Humboldt. "Pocotaroh" and his warriors"appeared destitute" in 1859. Severe overgrazing by emigrant stock left a wide zone of barren range land across the domain of this Northern Shoshoni band. After 1860 they began to resist emigrant

NINE

City of Rocks

In 1842, Joseph B. Chiles determined that a wagon road by City of Rocks and through Granite Pass was the most practical route from the Snake River and Fort Hall to the Humboldt. California bound emigrants began using this route the next year when large wagons began travel over the Oregon Trail. Later, those using the Hudspeth Cutoff from Soda Springs had to join this route and traverse Granite Pass. Salt Lake traffic joined this California Trail route a short distance beyond Granite Pass. "Two conspicuous spires were visible there, so all California emigrants had a chance to observe at least some marvelous granite formations in that area."[1]

Those emigrants going on to California, on Tuesday, 12 August 1862, headed south on the California Trail. In H.F. Swasley's letter, they

> now had a company of one hundred and twelve wagons, and the several trains joined for purposes of mutual defense. John Walker was unanimously elected Captain of the company. He made a selection of twenty well armed men, and mounted them on the best horses in the company, who acted as scouts, keeping in advance and closely examining the ravines and canons near the road. A similar number were placed in the

rear to guard against surprise from that quarter, while all who were not engaged in driving teams or stock were required to keep at convenient distance from each other on each side of the train. In this manner we started from Raft river.[2]

This included the Wilson Train with Jane Gould. "We only traveled half a day, camped on a creek, had the best of feed. Two or three other trains staid also. We have just heard that there has been a train waylaid on the Oregon road."[G]

Jane's sister-in-law, Lucy Gould Wyman, "Lou," washed cloths. In the evening they took in Mrs. Ellen Jones to travel with them. She is "one of the ladies of the plundered train, her husband goes in the wagon just ahead of us." The Jones' were married the morning that they left home for California. "Not a very pleasant wedding tour. Camped in the sage brush."[G]

Strangely, Jane Gould has no entry in her journal transcribed for that day. She does for the following day, when they were following Cassia Creek. "Thursday, August 14, Left our camp early to enter the kanyon but it was farther than we supposed, only got to the mouth of it at noon." This was near Conant. "Here we found some parts of wagons and yokes chains of emigrants that had probably been plundered last year."[*] They also found pieces of paper that had news concerning the war going on back East, "so it could not have been longer ago."

] Attacks at City of Rocks [

The previous year, on the night of 8 August 1861 the Harriman Train of seventy-five people in eleven wagons was

*See Volume II, *The Utter Disaster On The Oregon Trail*, Appendix IV, "1861 Attack on the Harriman Train.," and Appendix I, "Wagon Train Taken at City of Rocks, 1860."

attacked on the California Trail in the City of Rocks area. They were surrounded by forty persons—Indians led by some whites disguised as Indians. As the emigrants prepared for defense, the attackers "stampeded their stock, and that was the last seen of it, leaving on the ground the horseless wagons and their unhappy owners. The party, minus their stock," had to leave their wagons and belongings the next morning, packing on their backs as much of the necessities as they could carry. No lives were lost on either side—not a shot was fired by either party.

Indian attacks had occurred at City of Rocks this summer of 1862 too. Some during the first two weeks of August.[3] An encounter on the 3rd was reported by the Virginia City, Nevada *Territorial Enterprise*, in which a party of emigrants numbering 40 persons was supposedly attacked near City Rocks.

Five young ladies were carried off, and, it is thought, women and children in all to the number of 15. All the men were killed except one, who made his escape and arrived at Humboldt about the 20th of September. This train was called the "Methodist Train," which was not all together inappropriate, since the whole party knelt down and began to pray as soon as the attack was commenced. Every train which has passed over that portion of the route in the vicinity of City Rocks since the 1st of August has had trouble with the Indians.[4]

"Like many other such incidents reported at the time, this one may not have occurred."[5] There would have been more records of this if so many emigrants had perished.

On 6 August Indians attacked a party of seven packers from the Willamette Valley near the same place. One man, James Blue, was killed. Another, named Lee, had his pony shot from under him, but he and the remaining six escaped by breaking through the Indian ranks. They had to leave everything to the

Indians. They had only a little bacon for food the next four days. These packers had been to the Salmon River mines before returning to the Willamette Valley.[6]

Around 8 August, the Smith Train from Warren County "met a worse fate. All eleven wagons of this group, along with sixteen horses, were taken and five persons were killed. The survivors, left with no provisions were saved by Mormons who found them wandering near their settlements to the south."[7]

A train of 29 wagons from Linn and Hardin counties, Iowa had come over the Lander cut-off. This group included 45 men and fared better than the others when they encountered some of Pocatello's band on 9 August.[8]

They were attacked at noon at the mouth of the City of Rocks canyon by from 75–100 Indians. Some Indians were mounted and armed with good guns that shot accurately three hundred and fifty yards. They immediately corralled their wagons with the teams inside and threw up defensive ditches. The 45 head of loose stock was left outside.

The Indians tried twice to get the cattle, but were repulsed in the first attempt. The second time they were successful and "went about three-quarters of a mile away and had a great dance over it." The Indians harassed the circled wagons the remainder of the day and sporadically throughout the night.

Next morning the Indians held a council on the bluff, and "while thus parleying a part of the men in the train went out on horses, followed by some on foot, and drove the Indians over the ridge." The packers suffered only two wounded but lost their loose cattle.

] The Walker Train Continues [

After viewing the abandoned wagons of the 1861 attack on the Harriman Train, the Walker Train continued up the canyon of Cassia Creek.

After going up the kanyon about four miles we came to a wagon that had been stopped. There was a new harness or parts of one, some collars and close by we saw the bodies of three dead men top of the ground, they had been dead two or three weeks. Some one had been along and thrown a little earth over them, but they were mostly uncovered again. One had his head and face out, another his legs, a third his hands and arms. Oh! it is a horrid thing. I wish all the Indians in Christendom were exterminated. We did not get through the kanyon and were obliged to camp in a kanyon with the mountains on every side.[G]

In his letter H.F. Swasley had the day (Thursday) wrong: "Wednesday we passed a place where a wagon had been robbed and burned; here we found the bodies of five men murdered, and almost entirely denuded of flesh. They were, doubtless, returning Californians." (The Indians often opened emigrant graves to remove the clothing.) Swasley did not mention if they buried the dead. He must have been referring to the previous attacks at Massacre Rocks when mentioning that:

This night we were attacked again, but the night was dark, and none of our party were wounded; some of the stock was out of the corral but under the cool directions of Captain Walker, we got them all safely in, and then whenever the flash of a gun could be seen, our fire was directed to it. Several rounds were fired, but without any apparent effect, while the savage war-whoop served to keep us wide awake. At last a loud shriek from our besiegers, and the sudden cessation of their fire led us to believe that we had given some important Indian a severe wound. We were troubled no more that night, nor in fact any more from that time, as they were doubtless convinced that the vigilance with which Captain Walker guarded all points was more than they bargained for, and it is owning to his prudence and bravery that we had no further trouble, as we could every once in a while see Indians on the adjacent hills watching us, while their signal fires gave us warning that they were constantly in our vicinity.[9]

Early the next morning, the 15th, they "were aroused at one o'clock by the firing of guns and yelling of Indians answered by our men." Captain Walker called out, "Come on you red devils." It did not take Jane long to[G]

dress for once. I hurried for the children and had them dress and get into our wagon, put up a mattress and some beds and quilts on the exposed side of the wagon to protect us. The firing was from the willows and from the mouth of the correl. There were two other trains with us, there are one hundred and eleven wagons of all and two hundred or more men. The firing did not continue long nor do any harm. Our men shot a good many balls into the willows but I presume they were not effectual. We sat and watched and waited till morning, yoked the cattle and turned them out with a heavy guard and several guards to clear the bushes, cooked our breakfast and started.[G]

"There were ball holes through two or three wagon covers." A horse, a filly, belonging to the emigrants in a wagon in the Thompson Train was hit. "Two men felt balls whiz past their faces." An arrow was found near the opening of the corral. The trains traveled only a half a mile or so before eight or ten Indians were seen coming[G]

out of their hiding places on ponies and to our camping
place to see, I suppose, if they had lamed or killed any
men or cattle. The Capt. had plenty of scouts out and
an advance and rear and side guards. We nooned in a
little valley but kept our eyes open to all that might be
hidden in the bushes and behind the rocks. Camped by
the side of a mountain, near us on one side was a creek
with willows on it, on the other a deep gulch made by
the rain. The Newburn and Thompson Trains camped
and corelled with us the Capts. stationed picket guards
in the ditch and on the sidehill. In the night we were all
startled by the bark of the kiota which sounded very
much like the Indians when they attacked us last night.
The alarm gun was fired which awakened us all, after a
while we concluded it was the wolves and went to bed.
Most of the train slept under the wagons, set up flour
sacks and all manner of stuff. We hung up a cotton
mattress and some quilts and slept in the wagon. It is
not an enviable situation to be placed in, not to know at
night when you go to bed whether you will all be alive
in the morning or not. Came in sight of the City of
Rocks.[G]

The next day, Saturday, 16th, left early, entered City of
Rocks canyon and followed it up between high hills among the
rocks.

Passed by the City of Rocks, it really has some of the
appearance of a city at a distance. This has always
been known as the worst place for Indian troubles ...
Some of the rocks are covered with names from 1852
up to the present year. I don't think there has been
more than two trains through ahead of us. Did not stop
for dinner, in the afternoon there came up a thunder
shower, a real hard one. We had to pitch the tent in the

rain, it was quite a rarity, 'twas much pleasanter after it was over. It looked strange, the clouds seemed to lie on the mountains. They dug trenches again and had picket guards.[G]

Sunday, August 17 ... Came to Goose Creek this afternoon, went up it two or three miles, were obliged to camp on it near willows and close by hills, dug trenches again. Dug a deep hole on one of the hills for the pickets to stand in. Were not molested.[G]

Two days later the emigrants did not camp until nearly dark, so had to get supper by candlelight. The Goulds were able to let the tent remain standing overnight for the first time for a week. They could not before as Captain Walker thought a tent would give the Indians a good chance to creep up behind it. "They say that we are out of the Snake Nation for which I am truly grateful."[G]

The California-bound emigrants were then in Nevada, heading for the Humboldt. They had left the land of the Northern Shoshone and Chief Pocatello's Northwestern Shoshoni band. However, they were then in the land of the Western Shoshoni, also called Snakes and The Digger Indians.

Thursday, August 21, The road was rough some of the way, some steep hills to pass over. We saw several Indians today for the first time, they were Snakes. One of them said that he was chief. Three of the men in the Newburn train burned their wigwams in their absence, they came on at noon, were very indignant about it and wanted pay for it. Capt. Walker told them who it was that burned them, they got quite a good deal of bread and bacon from different ones from our camp. After being in trouble with them for so long we were glad to let them be friendly if they will. Albert, Lucy, and I went a short way from the road and got our arms full of currant bushes laden with fruit, both red and white. We ate what we wished and had nearly two quarts to eat with sugar for supper, they were really refreshing.[G]

Traveling along the Humboldt the Wilson-Walker Trains met the Northern Paiutes. On 3 September, Jane Gould noted that "There are numerous Indians around, they are Pah-Utahs, pronounced (Pa yoot). They are more intelligent than those we have seen heretofore." On the 5th the wagon train[G]

stopped early for dinner on the Humboldt. Here we are obliged to separate, some of the train go the Honey Lake Route, and some the Carson river route. We and 24 others go the latter one. The Capt. goes with the former. We seem like a family of children without a father. We think he is the best Capt. on the road. Some could hardly refrain from shedding tears, at parting tears came into the Capt's eyes as he bade them goodbye.[G]

The next day those heading for Carson City again stopped for noon by the river. There the men gathered and elected a new captain, named Wood. Jane Gould thought "he will be a good one, he and his wife have been through once before. He was Capt. when he went before. There were twenty or thirty Indians came in last night from Salmon River mines. They could most all speak English quite well, they live in Humboldt City. They say there is no gold in Salmon River mines."[G]

The Goulds came within three miles of Carson City on 22 September but passed on by. The next day other emigrants arrived in Carson City, in the recently created Nevada Territory. The city's newspaper, *The Silver Age*, reported those arriving "overland were S.B. Smith and family of Keokuk, Iowa, S. Johnson and family, J. Oswalt and family, and John Accord and family of Shelby county, Missouri

—altogether 17 persons, with four wagons drawn by mules and horses in fair condition." This 1 October edition of the paper contained an account of the attacks on emigrant trains at Massacre Rocks. This account was reprinted in other newspapers.[10]

The Goulds arrived near Stockton, California on 5 October 1862. From Stockton, where Jane's diary ended, they moved to Lexington, Santa Clara county. Albert died within a year. Jane re-married, to Levi Tourtillott 20 February, 1864. They remained in California.[G]

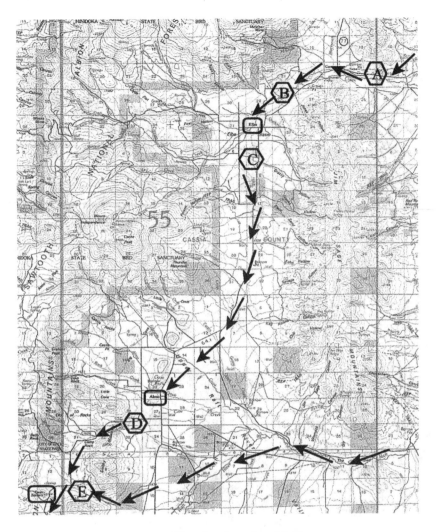

City of Rocks Attacks–1862

A. 8 August 1861, Harriman Train attack. **B**. 14 August, Walker Train discover bodies of five murdered men. **B-C.** 14–15 August, Walker Train attacked. **D**. 9 August, Mouth of City of Rocks Canyon attack. **E**. 12 September, California miners attack began on Salt Lake Road and continued east. Elba, to the north, Almo, and Twin Sisters to the southwest are **circled**.

Oakley ID 1:100,000 scale topographic map. Scale: vertical grid lines = 5,280 feet or 1 statue mile. Arrows indicate California Trail and Salt Lake Road. (Compiled by Author.)

Cassia Creek Canyon

Looking southwest on Idaho-77 highway toward the entrance to Cassia Creek Canyon. The California Trail followed along Cassia Creek and through the canyon. Inside the canyon the Walker Train passed by where the Harriman Train had been attacked the previous year.

Photo by Author, 2 April 2008.

Elba, Idaho on Cassia Creek

Looking north with Elba on the left and Cassia Creek flowing into the canyon area in the distance to the right. The Walker Train found the graves of five men by the creek toward the middle of the photo.

Photo by Author, 2 April 2008.

TEN

Attacks Near City of Rocks

Not all traffic on the emigrant roads headed west. Not far from the dry Honey Lake in northern California, fifteen men met at Lassen's Meadow and formed a company to head east. Some of them were from California, some from Carson City, Gold Hill, and other places in the Washoe area of Nevada. Some of them were bound for Denver and the balance for Missouri and other states where they had formerly lived. They left on the 3rd of September. If these men met the part of the Walker Train traveling the Honey Lake road, they must not have stopped to visit. Otherwise they would have been apprised of the danger from Indian attacks in the Snake country.[1]

The Salt Lake City *Deseret News* reported, "The company were all mounted, well armed, and had four pack in addition to their riding animals." They arrived at the junction of the California Trail and Salt Lake road, near City of Rocks, on the evening of 11 September and camped. The next morning they traveled but a mile or two on the Salt Lake road when they "heard the lowing of cattle, which led them to suppose that a company of emigrants were encamped near by, and, on descrying a smoke, produced by camp fires, a short distance from the road, some two or three men rode towards it for the purpose of purchasing some meat, if possible, of which they were in want."[2]

They had not gone far before they discovered that the smoke was from an Indian camp. They met some of the Indians "who appeared very friendly, among whom was their chief or leader." The two or three men saw

> a very large herd of cattle some four or five hundred head, nearby, which the chief said belonged to him and his band, they made known their wants. The chief told them that if they would go into his camp he would sell them all the beef they wanted. They did not mistrust that there was anything wrong till they had rode on a short distance further, when the chief asked one of the men if he was captain, and being told that he was not, the chief requested them to go back to the road and tell their captain to come up to his camp with all his men, and they should have all the meat they wished.[3]

The men returned to the company, but mistrusting the Indians did not go to their camp. They "thought it prudent to increase the distance between them and the wily red men," so continued on their way. They "had not gone far before they were fired on from the road side, upon which they started at full speed, followed by from thirty-five to forty Indians, mounted on good horses and well armed, and by a much larger number on foot, A running fight was kept up some twenty miles, during which all their horses were wounded, but only one man was hurt, and he but slightly."[4]

When these emigrant packers reached a branch of Raft river, called De Cassure creek, they had to abandon four of their horses. Two others also gave out which dismounted two of the party. So they went up into a canyon and endeavored to gain a position among the rocks, where they could defend themselves, as to proceed would be certain death to all who would be unhorsed, while the savages continued their pursuit, which they would in all probability do until the last man should be killed; but the Indians anticipated their movement, and before they reached the rocks three of their number were killed. From that time which was about the middle of the day, they fought the Indians, who swarmed around them thickly till after dark during which time another man was killed and four wounded, two mortally.[5]

By about 8 or 9 in the evening, the Indians had gained possession of the animals so "most of the Indians drew off, whooping and singing hideously." Soon after that the "seven men who were unhurt with the two who had each an arm broken, left their position just as the moon was rising." They took with them the two who were mortally wounded and carried them down to the bank of the creek, where they placed them side by side. As life in the two "being nearly extinct," they were left while the other nine "moved slowly and cautiously" in the direction of the settlements in Box Elder County, Utah Territory. "They were five days without food, and fortunately met a large company of emigrants some six miles beyond Bear river." The emigrants were headed for the Humboldt River and gave some food and relief for the horseless packers.

Samuel Riley was one of the two wounded men who escaped. He and two others who escaped named Jackson and Grant, returned with that emigrant company, "who had some thirty wagons and about eighty armed men. The other six, C. McBride, J. Andrews, James White, Eli Wilkinson, —— Lawson, and Johnson Foster, the latter wounded in the arm," went on to Brigham City. They later went on to Salt Lake City, "where they will remain a few days, and then proceed on their way to the east."[6]

The above encounter was reported in the Salt Lake City *Deseret News* on 24 September 1862. The information was confirmed by Charles McBride, formerly of Kentucky, and John Andrews. These two had come into Salt Lake City from Brigham City as passengers by the northern stage coach.

> The Indians, in addition to their horses, blankets, etc., got a considerable quantity of ammunition and most of the arms with which the company were well supplied. How many of the Indians were killed and wounded was not known, but many of them were seen to fall.
>
> The names of the killed, as given by Mr. McBride, were John Comer, whose relatives reside near Fulton, Callaway county, Mo, John Sharp, from Callaway county; Mr. Goodman, from near St. Louis; Joseph Snow, of Napa Valley, Cal.; William Davis, of Stockton, Cal., and Benjamin White, from Missouri or Arkansas.
>
> This is reported to have been the fifth or sixth company of emigrants, some of them large and having a great amount of stock, which has been attacked and used up in that vicinity within the last six or eight weeks by the same band, as supposed.[7]

The Salt Lake City *Deseret News* had more information on the encounter near City of Rocks on 11 September. The statements made about the affair came from Mr. McBride and others of the party. They, fortunately, had made their escape. Their report of the attack and escape of the survivors was corroborated. What they said was substantially true and correct, with the exception that there were only two of the party killed during the fight, and six wounded, two of whom were able to come away with those who left the battle-ground that night—two were left, as stated, supposed to be mortally wounded, and the other two, severely wounded, had concealed themselves in the brush or among the rocks where they remained unapprised of the departure of their comrades in the dark, who had good reasons for believing that they were dead. One of the four thus wounded and left was subsequently found and killed by the Indians. The other three are reported to be yet alive, having been rescued, after many days of severe suffering, by the company of emigrants under Capt. Price, who were met by McBride and those with him, at, or near, the Malade.[8]

The survivors of the attacked party met Captain Price's train seven days after the fight at the Malad River crossing. While the others went on toward Salt Lake, Jackson, Reilley and Grant, joined Price's train and went back to the battlefield with him. During the second night after they were attacked Goodman and Sharp, two of the wounded men who were supposedly killed, came into the Price Train camp

almost overcome with starvation and exhaustion. These men were badly wounded, one of them, Goodman, having been shot through one of his lungs; they had tasted no food for nine days and nights except rosebuds; had lain hidden in the willows on the bank of the stream every day and traveled on foot every night, half clad, although the weather was so cold that ice froze to the thickness of half an inch and the ground was covered with a white frost. In this way they had managed to drag themselves about twenty miles from the scene of conflict.[9]

Goodman and Sharp told Price's party that two wounded men, White and Comer (or Komer) were still in the vicinity of the battle-ground. Eleven horsemen were immediately sent to bring them to the camp and

> reached the spot before daylight, where they found Comer stowed away in the willows. He had remained there nearly ten days, subsisting, or rather starving gradually, on rose-buds, unable to get away, and tortured by the pains of nine bullet wounds, added to which was the suffering he experienced from the bitter coldness of the weather. White had remained exposed where he fell, during five days and nights, when a party of the Indians returned and killed and scalped him. Comer was placed on a sheet and carried about five miles by the horsemen. Here they stopped until the train came up. After the three dead men had been interred, the train moved on. Comer went on with the company to Virgina City, the other two, Goodman and Sharp, stopped at Unionville, Humboldt county.[10]

The men composing the company attacked "are represented to have been seceders, or sympathizers with the Confederate cause, and their misfortunes and sufferings have not been much lamented by their acquaintances in California and Nevada, professing to be of the Union faith."

When the Price Train left Brigham City, U.T. "fears were entertained that they would, like many others, be attacked by the hostile natives while en route and perhaps roughly handled, but it appears that, with one exception, they were not molested by the blood-thirsty revengeful red men." On 22 September,

> while resting at noon, a few miles beyond City Rocks, the company was fired into by a party of eight Indians,

and a young man named George Kauffman, from Nebraska, was wounded in the head, from the effects of which he subsequently died.   The Indians were pursued, but, being better mounted than their pursuers, they escaped the punishment they deserved.   They were well-armed with long range rifles, taken from emigrants.   Capt. Price thought that the chief of the band, from his style of dress, and manner of riding, belonged to that meanest breed of Indians which the world has produced—renegade white men.[11]

The attacks on Oregon Trail emigrant trains above Massacre Rocks and groups on the California Trail at City of Rocks, and other incidents, was Pocatello's band retaliation for a long sequence of attacks by emigrants, a few of whom had gone out shooting Indians along their route west through Shoshoni lands.   This led to military retaliation against a Shoshoni winter camp, which included some of Pocatello's band, by Colonel Patrick Edward Connor's California volunteers at Bear River, north of Franklin, Idaho 29 January 1863.

A series of Shoshoni treaties followed before another year's emigration reached Pocatello's country. By that time, southern Idaho had gained a large permanent population in a mining region that had not been occupied in August, 1862, and Indian relations entered a new phase with a constant stream of freight and stage traffic along roads that had been used only a few weeks each year by emigrants.   Systematic attacks against emigrant trains came to an end with Pocatello's resistance to Oregon and California trail migration in 1862.[12]

By 1868, Pocatello decided that his band would be better off settled on Fort Hall Reservation, and he arranged for a Bannock Creek home. After that, City of Rocks no longer had an Indian population. Pocatello died in 1884.[13]

Miners Attacked City of Rocks, on Salt Lake Road

12 September 1862

Killed

† William Davis	Stockton, Cal
† Joseph Snow	Napa Valley, CA
† Benjamin White, scalped	Missouri or Arkansas

Wounded

John Comer (Komer), 9 bullets, left behind	Fulton, MO
Johnson Foster, arm	
Mr. Goodman, shot through lung, left behind	near St. Louis
Samuel Riley (Rielley), arm broken	
John Sharp, left behind	Callaway County, MO

Unhurt–7

J. Andrews
—— Grant
—— Jackson
—— Lawson
C. McBride
James White
Eli Wilkinson

George Kauffman of Price Train, shot 22 September 1862 beyond City of Rocks, died later, from Nebraska.

† Buried by members of Price Train.

Miners Attacked City of Rocks.   (Compiled by Author.)

Rock Creek

Top: Looking north from US-93/Addison Avenue. **Bottom**: Looking northeast over Twin Falls' beautiful Rock Creek Park, from where Deadman Gulch joined Rock Creek. Here emigrant stock grazed. Photos by Author, 2 April 2008.

ELEVEN

Rock Creek

The emigrants continuing to Oregon left Raft River on 12 August, after burying Elizabeth Adams. "We have had a hard rocky road all day & through the most barren country we have yet seen if the thing were possible - The climate is growing more mild - nights not so cold - mosquitoes less & snow capped summits not so frequent."[J] Judson was not the only one describing the terrain. Bristol:

> The Snake River is tortuous as a snake's path in its course, and hence its name. It runs through a vast sage brush plain so destitute of forage and trees that scarce a Jack rabbit can find pasture and where a sage hen is rarely seen. In journeying down it on the south and west side we could only find feed for our hungry animals once in fifteen or twenty miles, when we came to small creeks on their way to the river. No buffalo or wild horses are found here. Now and then a deer or antelope is seen and half-starved wolves in hot pursuit.[B]

After traveling just one day from Raft River, Captain Kennedy was not able to travel, so the emigrants laid in camp for the day. Their cattle had become "peaceful and healthy" from some of the past days of not traveling.[HS] Judson had time to write,

> Capt K is reported worse & at the request of his train we conclude to pass a portion or the whole of the day here ... Our Capt kills a large Crane & some of our hunters discover a flock of bona fide Prairie Hens & get one or two of them - A couple out hunting find where an apparently large train of provisions has been robbed & demolished a year or more ago - Fresh Indian signs are plenty - It is reported that the Snakes & some other tribes are now holding or are about to hold a grand Council at Soda Springs about 50 or 60 miles south of us on the Cal road to consult on the expediency of "wiping out" all the emigration - We think their depredations for this season only just begun & that those who follow us will fare hard - We feel that we are getting past the worst places & shall with the assistance of a Kind Providence who has thus far shown clearly his guardianship & care go through unharmed - Capt K is this eve reported better & says we must travel tomorrow.[J]

After traveling seventeen miles the next day, the trains arrived at Goose Creek. The Reverend Bristol described an unusual occurrence:

> Not far from this stream, Goose Creek, we encountered a great cloud of winged ants. Several of us were on horseback just ahead of the train, when we saw beyond us, and stretching across our path, what seemed a layer of mist or a foggy wreath. It was perhaps forty rods long, thirty feet in height, and perhaps ten rods through. What could it be? Was it dust or fog or smoke? While

we were philosophizing we came against it, or it struck us, and then we knew. It was a cloud of flying ants. As they swept against us the whole train stopped. The horses snorted, thrust their noses down between their knees to brush them from their nostrils. Hundreds dashed against my face at a time. We could not open an eye nor see an inch before us. The air was hot and sickening. We plied our whips and spurs to our crazy horses, and holding our breath dashed headlong forward some ten or twelve rods, when we were through them. Had that swarm been a quarter of a mile thick, I suspect nearly every man and horse would have died. To say nothing about their picking our bones, we could not have endured that hot and intensely ant-scented air. The heat, I supposed, was from their breath and the warmth of their bodies. Whether such swarms of flying ants are common in this part of the plain I know not.[B]

Ants notwithstanding, the camp was a good one "amid a luxuriance of Wild Rye & plenty of grass for this country." The sportsmen of Judson's train shoot grouse and "many fall victims to their kill." An hour later the Kennedy ox train rolled in and corralled near the Bristol Train. Judson "had the huge snow banks of the Salmon River in range far on our right all day & some smaller range with less snow on the South much nearer." That would be the Sawtooths, Pioneer, and White Knob mountains to the north and the others, the South Hills and the Albion mountains. Their present force amounted to "65 wagons & 130 or 140 men I am glad to have another day pass with nothing concerning Indians to record - Hope to hear no more from them - I believe we shall not though some are confident we shall - We are always keenly on the alert & can not be taken by surprise."[J]

At one of these creeks our train and another spent a couple of day's. I went some distance down the brook, fishing for trout. A one-armed man not of my company went along, too, and went farther than I did. That night he did not come back! The next day his brother and some others went after him. They found his tracks and those of Indians, too, and saw where they had captured him and led him to the Snake River, where they crossed over, and they had to give him up! Poor one armed traveler over the Plains! He was never heard of afterward. "The Indian knows his resting place!"[B]

Judson listed two men named Phillips as being with the Bristol Train, James and Robert. Both were from Fairplay, Grant Count, Wisconsin. Captain Crawford, in describing the deaths at Massacre Rocks, "About the same time a Mr. Phillips left his train to go fishing, alone and unarmed, and was taken by Indians, and is supposed to have been killed. This happened near Goose Creek."[1] And also, "Near the same place and about the same time a Mr. Phillips left his camp, alone and unarmed, for the purpose of fishing, and is supposed to have been taken, as nothing has since been heard from him, and fresh Indian signs were found in the vicinity."[2]

The misconception that Phillips had been killed by Indians while fishing during the attacks near Massacre Rocks, and not at Goose Creek, was compounded by Daniel McLaughlin in a fanciful account:

One train which at the time was only 12 miles behind us had eight men and two women killed. A man named Phillips, from Denver, with only one arm, was taken prisoner by them and after keeping him two weeks they held a council near Big Hole. and put him to death in the following manner. Tying him to a tree. they cut off a joint of one of his toes. and then after going through a variety of whoops, yells and dances, cut off another, and so on until his ankles and knees had been severed; they commenced on his fingers until his arm was severed at the elbow. It took him two days to die.[3]

] A Case of Discipline [

Sherlock Bristol recounted an incident that occurred in the train one morning at about this time. It illustrated

the stern decision the chief officer of a train is sometimes obliged to exercise. As we were about to break camp one morning two men came to me with the complaint that their partner had refused to hitch his horses to the wagon, was packing his own baggage upon them, and about to leave his partners behind. I went at once and personally arrested him as he was about to proceed. He was mad and drew a revolver, but I had mine and demanded an explanation. From the testimony it came out that the three men were from Beaver Dam, Wis. That there they had agreed to go to the mines together. One was to furnish the wagon, another the supplies, and the third the team.[B]

Captain Bristol determined that so far each of the three men had fulfilled his part of the agreement. But "here our man of the horses broke his engagement, and swore he would leave the wagon and proceed with his horses." Bristol reasoned with the disgruntled man and "showed him that as a man he should stand by his engagement. To break it here meant the death of his two partners, unless others were more merciful than he." Finally Bristol told the man that the captain of the train "was bound to see to it that the contracts made at home, so vital now, should be carried out here!" But the man said Bristol[B] had no legal authority over him, and that he should do as he had a mind to. I said, "We shall see! Unpack your horses at once and hitch them to the wagon!" He raised his revolver and dared any one to lay a hand on his horses. I ordered every man to draw his weapon and sixty revolvers came forth quick. "Now stand away from him!" The clicking of revolvers being cocked, made one's hair stand on end. "Who will lay a hand on my horses?" said he. "I will," I replied, "if no one else will. Stop your threatening and unpack your horses. I give you just five minutes to decide whether you will do it. Every man level his pistol upon him, and if he raises his weapon fire on him!" Instantly he was covered by some sixty pistols. "Can I speak to Mr. So and So?" he asked. "Yes, but do your talking quick; this train is not going to be stopped very long by such conduct as this." The man went to him. In a whisper he asked: "Do you suppose they will shoot me if I resist?" The reply was: "Yes, they will put sixty balls through you! They will do it sure." These were several too many, and he threw down his weapon in disgust upon the ground and unpacked his horses, and we helped him put them onto the wagon. I left him with the remark, "See to it that this foolishness is not repeated again in this train!"[B]

Some days later, while the two were walking alone, the repentant man from Beaver Dam spoke to Bristol, "Captain, in general, I think I am an average man, but every now and then the devil gets into me and I am the biggest fool out. That is just what I was the other day. Now I want to ask you, as a favor, to take my money when I am in the mines, as fast as I get $50 and send it to my wife before I spend it in one of these fits of folly." Well, Bristol[B] partly agreed to do so, and from that time and for two years, we were warm friends. And when I returned some two years after I brought to Wisconsin $200, which I sent to his wife in Beaver Dam. An ounce of prompt and resolute decision is often worth a ton of vacillation and palaver.[B]

] Camp Delay [

After a quiet day of rest, Kennedy was better the next morning and the trains move on. The Kennedy ox train passed by the Bristol Train which was brought to a halt "by the sudden & severe illness of Mrs. Meeker." Then "the old Dutchman with a young wife finds one of his Iron Axles broken." The Bristol Train drove on a "short half mile" and camp for the day as Mrs. Meeker was unable to travel with the Kennedy Train continuing on. Later in the afternoon the H.R. Meeker team came up "also the Dutchman who has divided his load between Sapp & Durant & left his wagon." Henry Judson caught four "large trout from the rapids near & nearly or quite kill a large Rattlesnake several of which have been killed today - Many trout have been caught & if we had better grass would have a fine camp - This eve Mrs. M is better - I am on guard tonight."[J]

The men of the Kennedy Train shot one big deer and two antelope. The next day they "drove 10 or 12 miles and camped at noon on a nice creek to wait for several wagons drawn by horses that stayed behind on account of sickness and the wounded men. The horses travel much faster than the oxen."[RS]

That morning the Bristol camp had been roused at half past three. They remained in camp all day as Mrs. Meeker was unable to travel. Several more Rattlesnakes were killed near what was "supposed to be a den of them in the ledge of rocks along the rapids." They "have a call from one of Capt K's train which we think awaiting us 10 miles ahead - some are disturbed by the appearance in the distance of a man on horseback - It was probably one of our new men was out in that direction but not on horseback ... Our guest reports Capt K walking about this morning - This Snake river country with cultivation would sustain a numerous population - The soil seems rich & deep except in places where there are evidences of volcanic eruptions & the rocks are strewn over a considerable area."[J]

Both trains stayed in camp that Sunday, "Camp delay - Mrs. M is pronounced unable to travel & we are requested to wait another day At a meeting of the camp tis decided to do so much against the will of many though the vote to remain was unanimous when taken - We pass the day as best we can - Some kill Rattlesnakes one of which had the affrontery to cross our Corall & was about to be picked up by a yearling child of Freeman's when discovered by its mother - He soon paid for his temerity." John Hileman had the last watch that night. They were "ordered to be ready to leave at 6 1/2 am."[J]

The next day, 18 August, the Kennedy ox train was "still in camp waiting for horse train. Several men went hunting again this a.m., about three o'clock came in with a lot of nice game. The horse train pulled in about 4 o'clock. The sick were better. Everybody is glad they are better. We had a nice rain today. All are refreshed, but sad, since the fight Aug.10 with the Indians."[RS]

]   Rock Creek Encounter   [

The trains moved on the next day; the sick and wounded were slowly improving.[RS] They traveled "12 miles over a stony road mostly along a creek whose banks are precipitous rocks nearly all the way perpendicular & often 30 & 40 ft high - At noon we cross the creek."

The Rock Creek crossings are in the south part of Twin Falls, just south of the sugar beet factory. After crossing Rock Creek on 6 September, Medorem Crawford went three miles down the west bank to camp. "Good camps can be had for 4 miles further down the creek. The Great falls of Snake river are about 5 miles in a due north course from the crossing of Rock creek … The road follows down Rock creek for about 7 miles from the crossing."[4]

The trains traveled four more miles after crossing[J] with Captain Bristol, "Going ahead of my train in search of a camp I observed in the trail fresh tracks of Indians, also making for Rock Creek. They were but a few hours ahead of us. I went cautiously forward till I came to it. It ran in a deep canyon. Finding a path down into it, I camped there."[B]

Bristol did not mean that the emigrants camped in the deep Rock Creek canyon but nearby on the sage brush plain above. Three to four miles from the Rock Creek crossings placed the wagon trains along and above the creek into the present golf course in southwest Twin Falls, Idaho. Northwest of where they camped, west of the Magic Valley hospital and north of US 93/Addison Avenue, is the beautiful Rock Creek Park. Deadman Gulch entering Rock Creek from the southwest formed bottom land in the canyon where there was grass, trees, and brush on which the stock could graze. This was the avenue down which the stock were driven and is the present entryway into Rock Creek Park.

Henry Judson had his train camping again with the Kennedy Ox Train on the bank of Rock Creek "which grows deeper & here is not less than 60 or 70 ft to the water - Here we are to leave" Rock Creek the next day "2 miles from where it empties into the Snake river."[J]

The Indians were following and watching, but the emigrants had a camp site that the Indians could not attack and "get by with it." Robert Scott remembered camping near a creek in a deep canyon, which had a high rocky bluff on each side. There being only one way to get the stock down to water and grass, they separated the horses and cattle and herded them on a branch of the creek in a deep canyon. A heavy guard was placed with all of the stock. It was well protected from Indians with lots of willows in the bottom. The moon was very bright.[RS][HS] Bristol's

> suspicion of trouble at hand led me to look over the ground very carefully and determine what to do in case of an attack. When the time came to set the guards, I went to Ives, our famous hunter, and said: "Ives, I have a place for you tonight, I expect an attack before morning." "All right," he answered, and chose as his comrade for the night watch one John Henley, a young lawyer from Iowa City. I located them and returned to camp.[B]

About midnight, as Wednesday, 20 August began, with W.G. Ives and John Henley on guard with others, Bristol

> lay half asleep, my ear on the ground, I was aroused by a faint cry for help coming up from the canyon. Springing to my feet I seized my gun and rushed out to the guards who patroled the corral, and demanded whence that cry? The guard had heard none. Being the end of his beat, another guard came up; he, too, had heard no cry of distress. I was sure somebody was in trouble. While we talked another faint cry came up the trail. We hastened down. It was as dark as Egypt, and one of the guards stumbled over a prostrate body, and we turned and took up the body of Henley, the young lawyer, and bore it to camp. Limp it was and hung down heavily.[B]

When they reached camp, the doctor was called who applied restoratives. When Henley regained consciousness he said he had been wounded by an Indian arrow. He had come to tell the camp that Indians were after the stock. Apparently an Indian had slipped up and was concealed in the willows. It was then that the great arrow was embedded in his chest.[B RS] "It had penetrated six or eight thicknesses of his Oregon blanket, his coat sleeve and the fleshy part of his forearm, had then gone through his coat, vest and underclothes, and was apparently deep in his chest. All these garments were pinned to his person by this arrow. The blood was slowly oozing out."[B]

Bristol left Henley with the doctor, "and expecting he would soon die, I aroused the whole camp."[B] Word was sent to the other camp. Robert Scott said "The camp was wakened and the captain sent out 70 men to surround the canyon until sun rise, but they did not see the Indians."[RS] The Bristol camp was set in order for a fight. Bristol "called out my sage bush men and sharpshooters. Oh! how tardily they came, one by one. Repeated calls at the top of my voice scarcely hastened them. Every second was a minute to me! I wanted to fly to the side of Ives."[B] It was two o'clock when Judson and his mates were roused by Edward Wait who brought the intelligence to their tent that Henley "one of the Iowa City boys while on guard had been shot with an arrow & wounded in the arm near the shoulder - Of course we all turn out & while the bal of us stand shivering in the camp with the cold the Capt takes his 'Ambush men' & starts out to hunt the would be murderer - Very soon we hear a single shot from Ives who was in the ravine on guard ... All is then still till broad day."[J]

Captain Bristol described what had happened. He could not wait, and left "with half our number, leaving orders for the rest to follow. We crept stealthily along the bluff till near the place of attack. Here along the cliff overlooking Ives' position, I located the men, one here, one there, with orders to shoot any one without a hat. Wild Indians never wear hats. I myself crept down the rocks near to where I had stationed Ives. I knew if he discovered me he would shoot me for an Indian, but I was so anxious for him I wanted to be near him in case of an attack."[B]

Sherlock Bristol did not have long to wait. A bright flash of Ives' gun "burst upon the dark valley, the loud report rang and reverberated along the cliffs like a park of artillery." Some twenty feet in front of Ives "an Indian with half-drawn bow stood a second and then fell as the darkness closed in, and all was silence again. A few minutes and the dying warrior commenced striking out wildly with arms and legs." Bristol could hear distinctly the Indian's "motions and efforts to rise. By and by he began to roll over and then over again. After a time he reached the river bank, fell over, a loud splash, and then all was still again." [B]

For the rest of the night the men lay and watched the canyon. "As the first rays of morning began to modify the darkness," Captain Bristol[B]

descried an Indian on horseback, swaying back and forth, trying to make out just where we were. My shotgun, though heavily loaded, would hardly reach him, and I crawled back to where Hank Humphrey lay, and took him, with his rifle, to a point near the river, where we hoped to see the Indian. But he was gone. While we lay there together in the sage brush, I saw what seemed the outline of an Indian's body in a bunch of willows. The strong wind rushing through the narrow pass swayed the willows to and fro, and as they leaned this way and that, so leaned his body. Some time I watched it, when a sudden gust revealed him. Instantly my gun was up, but Hank knocked it down, saying, "Stop, Captain, it's an ox." A leap over the bank, and the Indian was out of sight.

Bitterly Hank reproached himself for this indiscretion, which had saved a murderer's life. I now called to Ives, and he came out from behind a rock, and when I told him where we had been since he sent wounded Henley up to the camp, he replied that he knew the Captain was not far off; just where, he could not tell. And when I told him how near I crawled down to him, he trembled to think of the danger ran. Believing that Henley was dead by this time, I believed I had a commission to destroy his murderer.[B]

Robert Scott remembered, "The Captain gave orders to go all through the rocks within a mile range. The sides of the canyon were covered with large broken rocks. We hunted about 1½ hours and were about to give up finding any Indians."[RS] Henry Judson: it was "broad day light when with the assistance of a dog the red skin is tracked & routed - Blood was found where Ives had fired & he had lain wounded on a green deer skin among the rocks & sage brush."[J] Captain Bristol asked his

lieutenant to go a little above and with some men cut off the retreat of the Indians, while I would cross over where we were, and follow up their trail. He objected, saying there might be hundreds of hostiles there. I said, Then I will go alone, and calling our company dog I jumped into the river, and following it up a dozen rods under the overhanging willows. I found where the Indians had crawled up the bank, and went up also, and pulled up the dog.[B]

To Bristol's surprise he found that two young men followed him—Charles McComb and Alexander Hargrave. "They would not see me go alone."[B]

When out of the river, we found the trail so difficult we had to break a path for the dog. Reaching the wall on that side, I saw the marks of a wet foot on a rock, which showed he had gone up the cliff there. I turned quickly to the right, looking on the ground as if still following the track. When we had turned a corner, and were out of sight, I said:

"That Indian went up the rocks where we first came to the wall. Hargrave, linger here several minutes, till McComb and I can go up this ravine and reach the top of the cliff. Then do you go back and follow the Indian up the rocks, rout him out, and we will have him."

But it took us longer to reach the summit than Hargrave expected, and he went back. Our Indian, seeing him come back alone, left his hiding place. Just then I appeared on the plateau. He was some forty rods off, and could easily have kept out of reach. He was armed with a bow and arrows, and when he saw me he shook his fists in my face, and ran to meet me. I, too, ran to meet him.

We were in full sight of a hundred men of my own train and Kennedy's, who saw us running together from the opposite bluff, and set up a universal shout. My train had great confidence in my coolness and marksmanship, and, I think, had no fear of the result, but wondered that while he ran fast I ran toward him rather slowly. The reason was, I wished to preserve my breath and steadiness of nerve.[B]

"Then one of the men found one Indian hiding under a rock in a hole near the top on the opposite side of the big hill from where" Robert Scott and the others were camped. "The Indian jumped out and ran."[RS] "As soon as discovered our men gave a shout & many shots were fired at the fellow - They gave chase."[J] The Indian came within eight or ten rods of Bristol, then turned to run away. The Captain raised his shotgun, and the Indian

> began dodging to right and left; but that did not prevent his receiving sixteen heavy shot in his back, just above the heart. His weapons fell out of his hands; he staggered, but laid hold of the sage brush with both his hands to hold himself up. McComb coming up, trembled so with excitement that he had to rest his rifle on my shoulder; but the ball flew aside from the mark. And now the firing began from the other side the river, and so thick the balls flew about me and McComb that I had to swing my hat and order them to stop.[B]

The Indian "made good use of his legs while the bullets whizzed after him."[HS] "We followed shooting at him for about 2 miles before catching him."[RS] At the end of about two miles the pursuers overtook the exhausted Indian.[J] Hamilton Scott "being shorter of breath than some others, fell behind about a half a mile" when the men surrounded the Indian.[HS] "In ten minutes fifty men had crossed the river, come over the bluff, and surrounded the wounded warrior."[B]

Henry Judson stated that when they neared the Indian "he begged as well as he could by throwing up his hands etc but nothing could save so audacious a scoundrel—Several pistol shots were fired into his breast without his falling & when the foremost man came up with him he showed fight with his fists & his brains were beaten out with a gun barrel."[J] "In his dying moments he struck a man and knocked him nearly a rod." The man said to Bristol, "His stroke was like the kick of a horse."[B]

John McGuire (probably a relative of Mrs. Kennedy) was misidentified as "McQuire" when Robert Scott stated that the Indian "had been shot about 16 times and was weakened from loss of blood and he fell. A young man named McQuire was nearest the Indian, shot all his ammunition into him and he still

showed fight and McQuire struck him on the head with his
six-shooter and killed him."[RS]

Judson described the dead Indian as "almost naked … He
appeared to be about 25 yrs of age & was a stout well built
fellow."[J] Bristol concurred: "This Indian was a monster in
size. His neck and shoulders were like those of a bullock. We
afterward learned from friendly Indians that he was a big chief
among the Bannocks, that they regarded him as the strongest
man in the world. That at Fort Hall he whipped four men who
set upon him at once. They also gave us his name. I have
forgotten it, but it signified 'Big Thief.'"[B] Judson figured that
the Indians "had probably followed us a long distance
watching for an opportunity to shoot the guard slyly - take a
horse or two & gun & be off."[J]

Bristol was asked by the men who chased the Indian for
"the privilege of scalping him. This I refused. But unknown to
me, they did it."[B] "We scalped him and left him laying there;"
Robert Scott "got some of the scalp." Hamilton Scott, who
had lagged behind in the chase, did not go on to see the dead
Indian, but one of the boys gave him a piece of the dead
Indian's scalp.[HS]

> The sun was now perhaps nearly one hour high and as
> we were going on our way back to camp we discovered
> what we took to be a heavy dust rising east of us which
> we concluded was a band of Indians who were coming
> to the rescue of their unfortunate comrade which had
> fallen in our hands and whom was slain. You ought to
> have seen us go. I think we went back to camp in less
> time than we went out, however, as we neared the
> camp, we got brave and slowed down to a brisk walk.
> A little later we discovered that it was only a fog or
> mist raising from the water pouring over a falls on the
> Snake River.[HS]

After the emigrants had started back to camp and were a half mile away some of the other Indians came out and took the dead warrior away. The emigrants did not go after the Indians, "because we thought we got the one who shot our man" and so continued on to camp.[RS]

What remained of the scalp was presented to John Henley, "who survived, his chest not having been mortally pierced by the arrow."[B] "The wounded man is sick at the stomach but his wound not serious … We of course get a late start."[J]

"As we left camp that morning, Indians rose up out of the sage brush near our camp and ran to where the two Indians were killed, showing that they had been spectators of all that had passed."[B]

Judson: "Soon after leaving camp we discover 3 Indians searching the ground over - We judge from appearances etc. that they find the body of their comrade - We keep close to the Ox train all day which left camp ahead of us."[J]

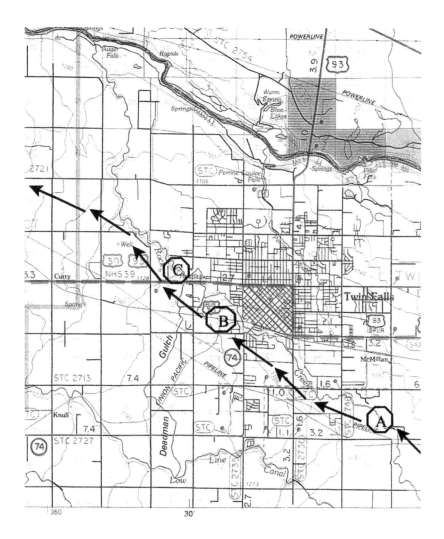

Rock Creek

A. Rock Creek crossing. B. Emigrants camped all along west side of Rock Creek where Twin Falls Golf Course is located. C. Flat bottom land in Rock Creek Park where emigrants grazed their stock. Deadman Gulch used to get stock from sagebrush plain down to bottom of canyon.

Twin Falls ID 1:100,000 scale topographic map. Scale: vertical grid lines = 5,280 feet or 1 statue mile. Arrows indicate Oregon Trail.

(Compiled by Author.)

TWELVE

Camp Discontent

The wagon train that Evan S. McComas was in traveled along the Oregon Trail three days behind the two separate trains led by Kennedy and by Bristol. On the evening of 21 August 1862, a trial was held in McComas' train about a stolen purse. That night "the Indians stole 4 head of cows from out of our drove." The thieves came close to the wagons and drove the cows away while four men were on guard. In the morning the emigrants decided to follow the Indians to regain the stock. The train was moved onto a hill to a stronger position Fifteen men, including McComas, volunteered to go and followed the Indians "about 12 miles up a deep canyon, looking for an ambush every minute, but could not overtake them." The volunteers got back to the train at sundown.[EM]

The next morning, the 23rd, after driving ten miles the train crossed Rock Creek, miscalled "Canyon Creek. Here we found where 8 Indians had come down the canyon before us." The train stopped for dinner and then traveled eight more miles while eight of the emigrants followed the Indians. But the Indians went on down the creek below where the train camped.[EM]

This evening 7 men with pack horses came close to us, and rode on past us to camp, which looked very suspicious. We expect to see them again think that they are outlaws in connection with the Indians as this is no place for 7 men to be without more. The country here is a vast plain covered with giant sage, composed of burnt rocks and damned bad dust and inhabited by horned toads and rattlesnakes, and the damned Snake Indians. Passed by where Capt., Kennedays's train had killed 3 Indians & one man wounded on Aug. 20."[EM]

Ahead of McComas the Bristol Train, with Judson, passed by the Thousand Springs on the day they left Rock Creek.

At noon we reach a place on the bluff where the river is accessible though a mile & a half distant & down a terrible hill - It is a singular & really romantic spot - Opposite us the rocks rise 600 ft perpendicular from the river - except a steep slope down to the waters edge - 3 huge Springs come out of the walls & foam & tumble to the river making pools the waters of which can be distinguished from the river for a long distance after reaching the same level - Some party probably Indians build a campfire some think a signal to other parties near the most distant springs.[J]

The trains had not proceeded far that day "before the smoke of signal fires began to ascend from hilltops in different directions around us, some of them ten miles distant! And then we knew well the whole Bannock tribe was upon us." Bristol and most of the people in his train and Kennedy's[B]

were badly scared. We saw Indians on horses dashing over the hills at full speed to carry the news to the scattered warriors. The view I took of the situation differed widely from the rest. I said, "We are safer now than ever. They are mad, but they are scared, too. Their invincible chief attacked us by night but was outwitted and killed; he and his companion. They will hover around but run when we steal through the brush to get at them." And so it proved. They followed us perhaps 200 miles but did not dare attack us.[B]

The two trains drove eighteen miles that day, a long hard and dusty drive in the afternoon. Just before sundown they descend a long hill and camped on the bank the Snake River.[J]
[HS]

5 Indians are discovered on the opposite bank—The stream here is narrow & rapid—rolling over huge rocks—We get our suppers—make our bed in the open air & lie down with the expectation of being roused to fight or hunt Indians before morning—Showers are hovering around—the wind blows—sand flies & altogether tis a most disagreeable camp[J]

Thursday Aug 21st—No disturbance last night—Up early—Stock taken back a mile or so to find grass—Ox train ordered to leave before sunrise but don't get off - 5 friendly Indians visit our camp bringing Salmon to "Swap."[J]

"Friendly Indians came to camp this morning with fish to trade also some came at noon. They tell us that we are out of the Snake tribe."[HS]   "We think they were following us and looking for a chance for revenge. We think they saw there were too many of us to attack. That was the last we saw of them."[RS]   Henry Judson thought these Indians were "tolerably good looking fellows—The Ox train leaves a wagon & in the course of the day unyoke a cow—roll her out of the road & drive on."[J]

We noon about a mile west of Capt K's train & part of our train a qr of a mile still farther on—on acc't of grass & all on the same stream - called Salmon Falls river—It is now about 2 rods wide & in depth up to the wagon bed—Near us on the opposite side of the river is a small Indian village of perhaps a dozen "Wickeyups" of friendly "Shoshonees"—One visits us & assures us that we have passed all the bad Indians—behind us they are very bad —They recently stole his peoples ponies & shot one of his men in the hips - before us all are friendly—I make a "swap" with an Indian boy—give him a fish hook for a hair line—They are more primitive Indians than I ever expected to see using still the flint head arrows etc.^J

Salmon Falls on the Snake River, "Tis very pretty to look at & a favorite camping place as well as resort of Indians - Two or three families are now here who live by 'swapping' with the emigrants - They catch a great amount of Salmon wading out on the falls & spearing them - One fellow this eve brought in 15 which would average 20 lbs in wt - a butcher knife or half dozen fish hooks buys one & a couple of biscuits gets a large slice."^J

We meet here 7 Cal packers or rather they are from Oregon - They say that the indians are friendly below - that we are 180 miles from Ft. Boisie by this route but can get there in 100 by fording the Snake & going down on the other side - They say a large party of Flat heads are near us on the north & a train one day in advance of us on our road - They tell nearly the same story of the mines as the last party we met - We are thinking that we are getting pretty well through the hostile Indian country & lie down tonight with a feeling of greater security than we have for a long time enjoyed

- A train of U. S. soldiers from Ft. Wallawalla are on the road this way & we shall probably meet them in 2 or 3 days - They exert a good influence here even if they are not called upon to fight - I think we already see it - We think if there are any trains behind us that they will have a rough time ... The roar of the fall is a splendid lullaby.[J]

The Jack Train reached Salmon Falls and the Thousand Springs four days after the Bristol and Kennedy Trains, on 25 August. That morning "an Indian came into camp on his pony. Some were in favor of shooting him, some not. He had come with 3 salmon to trade off." On Salmon Fall Creek "10 or 15 Indians came to trade off fish. Came 5 miles and then stopped 2 miles above Salmon Falls. Here the opposite side of the river is about 100 feet high in bank and a large river comes in about half way down the bank. It has sunk some place and breaks out here the same as a large springs. It is covered with rocks and falls in like the waters over a mill dam."[EM]

They had to lay over the next day as Mrs. Davis was sick. "Some trading with the Indians who are around camp most of the time."[EM]

The Bristol Train left Salmon Falls on the 22nd and drove about nine miles, found good grass, and stopped to let the stock graze. When about to start again, a messenger from the Kennedy Ox Train[J]

arrives requesting us to wait till they come up as the actions of the packers at last nights camp were suspicious - We have had our fears so much & often aroused that we suspect everything & everybody Our senses are all acute & on the alert at every sound & circumstance - Last night one of the guards saw two Mules leaving the Corral & thinking someone might be leading them fired his pistol & considerably alarmed some - We remain harnessed & ready for a start for an hour & a half & when many have become very anxious for their safety & not a little for our own we espy them at a distance slowly toiling on ... Tonight a comet is distinctly visible near the constellation of "Ursa Major."[J]

In Judson's journal, Saturday 23 August, "The stock having had no grass since yesterday noon are early taken out to feed - After breakfast - which some are late in getting we decide after a lengthy debate to remain here until Monday."[J] "We found some grass near this a.m. and stayed in camp. We are told we are out of the hostile Indians now. We are all glad for such good news. As we have had lots of trouble the past few weeks with these hostile Indians. We will camp here until Monday."[RS] Judson described some horse trading:

Three Indians on their ponies came into camp this morning & have been here more than half a day - Hurst bought one for flour etc. & Jack traded "Sam" for another one giving 8 shirt & 2 fish hooks "to boot" Fish hooks are a good currency & seem to be a legal tender - I have never been much in love with "Sam" have had little to do with him but still hated to see a bigger brute mount him & start him off to perpetual slavery - Poor fellow he has a hard life before him.[J]

Just after dark as Judson got into his "blankets a gun was fired at the foot of the first hill toward the river." A dozen or more emigrants[J]

soon assembled & learned from Mrs. Freeman that her husband & the young man "Billy" had gone down for water with a horse a short time before - Soon came another report & then Temple hallored to them & was told to "lie low" By & by they came up & reported that they had seen 3 Indians who skulked as soon as discovered - They left their horse - water & all & hurried up to the foot of the hill & fired to have the camp on the lookout for them - A pleasant prospect surely for being on guard tonight - As usual the last watch "Chubb" the pet is missing tonight - he went down with some other stock & no one specially to care for him & chose to stay all night - John thinks he is gone for good - Several other animals are missing having been left & lost in various ways Their chances are poor.[J]

Joe Sprott, "Jack" Humphrey, Hank Ryerly, and Judson were on guard for a long, quiet watch through the night. That was all of their household except for John Hileman. Sunday 24 August: "The horse that Freeman left with the water were found early & Chubb also came to light - Think he is safe as no Indian can get near him."[J]

"Had preaching at three o'clock by a Captain of the horse train who is camping near us."[HS] Robert Scott, "Had a Sunday of worship and rejoicing for being away from Indians. If the report is true. We had preaching by Rev. Bristol. Capt. Kennedy and the others need a rest. All are getting along very well now, and we are so pleased and everybody is happy." Several smaller trains had joined for protection to all from Indians. "... we took census of our train—now having 1800 people, 2300 head of stock, consisting of horses, oxen and milk cows. This was quite a camp meeting."[RS]

Judson: "The usual service was held today near Capt K's Corral & we had quite an audience of women - Capt Bristol preached one of his best sermons from Rev 3d 20th The usual choir did the usual good singing - Today I don for the first time my new bed ticking pants & feel really dressed up."[J]

John Hileman and "Jack" Humphrey, with a number of others, stayed with the stock that night on the bottom by the river. That saved one trip down the big hill and allowed an early start.[J]

On Monday, the 25th, they left Camp discontent with the Kennedy "Ox train having over an hour the start of us ... Terrible road for our stock - Our team is reduced to four Mules today - Ives taking a pair of them & with them 300 lbs of our load Jack puts his new Indian pony into Ives team also." The pony did not know what to make of it but was persuaded by a black snake whip "to go along tolerably well."[J]

The next day the trains passed a "guide board which says a party 12 days ago lost some stock by Indians & were obliged to burn some of their wagons." Joe Sprott and Judson met "2 Indians travelling with their packs on their ponies - Have passed several old deserted 'Wickeyups' - Not many Indians in the Country but ugly as ———" Ferdinand Roosevelt and William Shepard "lose a mule last night - She has been sick since Friday eve ... At night the stock is taken to the top of a high mountain for grass & is then guarded all night - We conclude to leave our heavy old wagon & make an arrangement with Ferd & Shepp to put our load on to their wagon - We immediately begin to carry out our plan & before dark the change is made & the old wagon run out" to one side of the road.[J]

THIRTEEN

Oregon Volunteers

The trains did not cross the Snake River at the Three Island Crossing but kept following along the river on the South Alternate route. Since Monday the Bristol Train lagged behind the Kennedy Ox Train. But on Thursday 28 August the Ox train was passed as it was detained by the illness of Dr. Collins. The trains passed by the 452 foot high Bruneau Sand Dunes, that Judson described as "some beautiful sand hills pure & clean as a snow bank & as fantastic in shape - We leave this valley by a long tedious hill & find on the top a table about a mile wide - As we near the western slope we are signalled by the Capt & some others ahead - good cheer - Soon we get sight of Keiser [sic] River valley green & beautiful & an involuntary cheer rises in each throat - We are still five miles from the stream & many rush ahead on foot."[J]

The Bruneau was probably named as early as 1818 by French-Canadian trappers that were with the Hudson Bay trapping party led by Donald McKenzie. The French "brun" means dark and "eau" means water. The name, Bruneau, was used by emigrants passing here in prior years, but James McClung called it "Kyser Creek."[JM] A week of the Hamilton Scott diary is missing, the pages torn out, 26 August–1 September.[HS] His brother, Robert, whose account was dated the following January, has only a long entry for 25 August and does not make another entry until 3 September. Robert does not name the location where they met the soldiers. Judson called the Bruneau "Keiser River." Sherlock Bristol was also confused. He called the Bruneau "Catharine Creek," which empties into Castle Creek just before that stream flows by Castle Butte and into the Snake River, twenty miles to the west. Bristol thought the Bruneau was the western limit of the Bannock range. The Indians were determined to make a stand there and

> sent forward a chief and three braves to lie in ambush, spy out our camp defences, and attack us with their whole force by night. Going forward to select a camp as usual, there went with me one [E.M.] Geiger. Passing through the willows which lined the creek. I observed fresh footsteps of Indians, and also a strong smell of Indians. With quickened step I hurried through and made for an open space some twenty rods square and sat down in the middle of it. Geiger coming up asked, "What's your hurry, Captain?" I said there are Indians there; I smelt them and saw their fresh tracks also.[B]

Some of the emigrants thought they saw a train in the distance coming toward them. They speculated "upon the probability of their being the expected soldiers or pesky Indians."[J] Bristol continued:

> In an hour or so the train filed down the long hill. Most of the men, eager for game, came rushing on ahead, gun in hand, and as they came near the willows spread out like a fan. In doing so they unwittingly surrounded the Indians, and seeing them hid in the bushes quickly took them prisoners and brought them to me. While I

was examining them and considering what to do with them, we were startled by the sound of a bugle approaching us from the opposite direction. Soon the advance guard of a regiment of United States soldiers and cavalry came filing around the hills! Hearing of the troubles on the plains, the United States Government had sent out from Oregon these troops to help the beleaguered emigrants.[B]

While Judson and some of others were bathing, their train came along. They crossed the Bruneau and went "into camp about a mile from the ford & such a camp - tis really refreshing to camp again on the bank of a fine gravel bed stream & on good green sward with wood & grass in abundance."[J]

The approaching train was 300 soldiers sent from Oregon to protect the emigrants and assist them to a settlement. "They have provisions for the destitute & are designed as a protection & relief to the emigration."[J]   Colonel Reuben F. Maury's command consisted of Companies A, B, and D of the First Cavalry Oregon Volunteers which was ordered out from Fort Walla Walla on 25 July. Some of the soldiers were to go on to Salmon Falls and await the arrival of Captain Crawford's emigrant escort which was bringing up the rear of the emigration.[J 1]

Brigadier-General Benjamin Alvord, Commanding the District of Oregon, apprised the Governor of Washington Territory, William Pickering, of the Army's special concern for the protection of the incoming emigration. General Alvord had heard that

Lieutenant-Colonel Maury's command of three companies of Oregon cavalry probably started to-day from Fort Walla Walla upon the emigrant road. Salmon Falls, half way between Fort Boise and Fort Hall, is the great haunt of the Snake Indians at this season for the purpose of fishing, and Colonel Maury's command will remain encamped in that vicinity as long as possible, not leaving there until it is necessary in order to return to Fort Walla Walla by the 1st of November. Mr. Crawford, of Oregon, with a guard of seventy-five men enrolled for the journey by order of the War Department, left Omaha early in June and writes Major Francis that he intends "bringing up the rear of the emigration." I have given no order to Colonel Maury about "bringing up the rear of the emigration," for that phrase with us is rather unsavory and unsatisfactory, as in the fall of 1860 a commander who supposed he brought up the rear of the emigration had the sorrow and mortification to hear of a massacre in his rear ... Colonel Maury is ordered if opportunity occurs to arrest and punish those Snake Indians who committed the murders of 1860.[2]

Much of Maury's force would operate from the Bruneau Valley as it and the Boise Valley were the only two places with enough grass to support the soldier's horses and mules for any length of time. Robert Scott did record that "While in camp here a company of soldiers came by going east to help other trains to get through the hostile Indians. We consider ourselves very lucky to get through, so far as well as we have."[RS] Judson observed that they were

booked to remain till Saturday morning if not till Monday - The Indians are ugly below & are constantly committing thefts & depredations   There is quite a body of the vagabonds a short distance above us on the Keiser [*sic*] & very soon after we had Corralled a dozen or so were seen coming toward us - They seemed aware of our movements but not of the soldiers - When they got near & discovered two or three soldiers in our camp they quickly dropped their bows & arrows in the grass & came forward without them - A mounted soldier made them return & get them & then started with 4 or 5 for their camp some two miles below he intended to examine them with their guide & interpreter but they gave him the slip on the way down by dodging into the willows - The rest remained but a short time in camp & stole off.[J]

When Colonel Maury's tent was pitched, he sent a squad of soldiers to Bristol to fetch the Indian prisoners. "On the way they skipped right and left and all four escaped. They soon rejoined their forces concealed behind the hills and told them that the game was up, there were too many of us now in the valley to be attacked. Their chagrin was great and they came out upon the hillsides in full view, and there they ran their ponies for full half an hour and thus worked off their wrath and gave vent to their vengeance. Then they slowly took the backward track and we saw them no more."[B]

The soldiers are a terror to them & their presence here is of great benefit to us - At least making us easy in mind if not preventing positive trouble - Notwithstanding the depredations on the road the soldiers have seen no Indians They have with them a man named Tomy who has met them & is returning to try & find a brother made captive this season not far from Salmon Falls - They have also a party bound for Deer Lodge valley prepared to ransom some children supposed to be held captive in that vicinity.[J]

The children referred to by Judson were undoubtedly the three Van Ornum girls and their brother, Reuben, who were taken captive when their family was atrociously murdered two years before at Farewell Bend. They were part of the Utter

wagon train that was taken in a prolonged two-day attack at
Castle Butte, 9–10 September 1860.* Zacheus Van Ornum was
working with the army, and others, to effect the rescue of his
nieces and nephew.

]   Encampment on the Bruneau   [

The next day, Friday, 29 August, Judson and company slept
late, "no hurry on a day of rest." After breakfast the military
camp moved up to a bend in the Bruneau a half mile above the
emigrants. "They make a very good appearance on their very
good horses - have about 400 horses - 30 Wagons & something
over a hundred pack Mules - The soldiers seem more intelligent & better behaved than the generality of soldiers are - Not
an Indian has been near our camp today."[J]

It was one of the hottest days the emigrants had experi-
enced on the trip. Late in the forenoon the Kennedy Ox Train
arrived and went into corral between the Military camp and the
Bristol Train. "Some half dozen of their men who were
driving a weak cow some distance behind their train a few
miles back were frightened by the appearance of a few Indians
at some distance & left their cow behind & ran." That evening
the Bristol Train voted to remain over Sunday.[J]

The emigrants spent Saturday tightening bolts, soaking
loose wagon wheels, shifting loads, re-setting tire rims, etc.
Judson thought they would leave here on Monday. "Powder
river is still ahead & is no doubt our destination   Shall all
regret leaving this pleasant camp & as much on acct of the
feeling of security we enjoy as for any other reason."[J]

For Sunday they had preaching in each of the three camps.
Judson went to the Military encampment passing Capt
Kennedy's "very quiet camp" on the way.[J]

---

*See Volume II, *The Utter Disaster on the Oregon Trail.*

I come first upon a party washing - plastering - lancing & otherwise doctoring a lot of poor galled mules which have been injured in packing - They are truly a woful (woeful) sight to behold - Next I come to the QrMasters Margin where a case of shoes is being distributed - then on through the camp & see a perfect beehive for industry.- Some mending - some washing - some fishing - some cleaning muskets & swords - some repairing harness etc. etc. etc. "ad libs"- At the upper end is the blacksmith - his forge and old Gun Carriage with a bellows in place of gun - a real Anvil on its natural block & his shop as large as Goldsmiths black- smiths ever was - He has plenty of work - Over 200 animals to keep shod - Then I pass around by the pack train Their packs neatly ranged in rows like cotton bales or perhaps more like sacks of corn & the animals closely ranked along one side - I am well paid for my visit & better than ever satisfied that a soldier's life is not the life for me - At 1/2 past ten we have a sermon by Mr. Bristol in Capt K's Camp The audience was a large & attentive one & composed of full delegations from the 3 camps ... We have quite a discussion this eve on the Question of moving on in the morning.[J]

]   Petition for a Soldier Escort   [

Bristol recalled, "As the time drew near when we were to continue our journey, a petition was gotten up for an escort of soldiers to accompany us to Oregon. Nearly every one signed it."[B] It was that Sunday that Judson noted "A petition quite numerously signed by both Capt K's train & ours asking for an escort through the dangerous country was today presented to Col. Maury."[J] Bristol:

It was presented by an able committee and well argued by a lawyer. Col. Maury, looking over the long list, said: "I don't see Capt. Bristol's name here?" The lawyer replied that he would not sign it. "Why not?" said Col. Maury. One of the committee said Capt. Bristol was a man without personal fear, and would run risks no sensible man could approve. The colonel called an orderly and bade him bring me to him. When I came, he said: "I see your name is not on this petition for an escort. Will you let us hear your reasons for not thinking an escort should be granted?" I replied that my principal reason was that I thought the trains behind us would be in greater danger than we. That his whole force would be needed between this place and Fort Hall. That, if we would act the part of men, keep a good lookout, keep close together and select defensible camps, we would go through all right. Besides, if an escort were given us, our men would become careless and lean wholly on the soldiers for defence. But if we went without them, we would all be watchful prepared, and therefore safe. Turning to one Capt. Crawford— the senior captain of the regiment—the colonel asked: "What do you think of that, Capt. Crawford?" "That is sensible," he replied, and half a dozen other officers assented also. The colonel then said to the committee:

"The view presented by Capt. Bristol is not only sensible, but it is patriotic. I agree with him entirely, and if you will heed his advice to rely on yourselves and keep close together, you will go through safely. I cannot give you an escort."[B]

Colonel Maury, Judson recorded, says "that he thinks our two trains capable of taking care of themselves." Captain Bristol did not sign the petition and some of the petitioners

thought that spoiled their chance for an escort by his represen-
tations and indifference.[J]

> The meeting broke up. The committee went out swear-
> ing mad and poured out their wrath without measure
> upon "Bristol's dare-devilism which had deprived us of
> an escort, and, no doubt, would prove the ruin of us
> all." And for once I was thoroughly unpopular, even in
> my own train. I offered to resign and have the train
> choose another captain. But no one seconded my
> suggestion and no one seemed to covet the privilege of
> running the risks I took every day in going forward and
> selecting our camps.[B]

Upon hearing the next morning, Monday, 1 September that
another woman was quite sick in the Kennedy Train it was
decided that they should not move. As it was voted not to
start, a renewal of the petition question took the attention of
some, "much to the disgust & chagrin" of Captain Bristol.
Charles M. Harrison, John C. Henley (a lawyer), E.A. Temple,
H.R. Meeker, and Henry Judson were appointed as a committee to wait upon Colonel Maury and learn what he could or
would do. The Colonel still declined to do anything, "his only
argument being that the two trains combined were strong
enough to resist any attack" that they might meet.[J]

Colonel Maury with two Companies, a small pack train,
and twelve wagons left about 7 o'clock for Salmon Falls.
Captain Harris was in command of the remaining soldiers, so
the committee renewed "their petitions to him for an escort of
20 men & with a fair prospect of success when news arrived of
the arrival of two trains from the East - They proved to be a
small train from Iowa & a small train from Denver combined
& they report having seen the dust rising from another
advancing train as they were leaving Salmon Falls."[J]

Robert Scott, "While camped here another train came up, and they had more trouble than we did in getting through the Indians, lost a lot of men and were robbed, had several hard fights. Said there was still another train behind them. Some of the soldiers will camp here a few days with us and the others will go east to get other emigrants and help them through. There are now four trains camped here. Some of them have come on and left a part of their train behind. They will wait here for them to come up.[RS]

] McComas In the Carseley Train [

Three days before arriving at the encampment on the Bruneau, the train that Evans McComas was in had a pony stolen by Indians. The next day, 30 August, their Captain, William Jack, resigned. After a "good deal of talk and jaw," William Carseley was elected captain. Two of "our boys tried to come down the river in a wagon box & got wrecked and had to swim ashore. One of them lost his pants."

The next day, Sunday, they "passed large sand mounds to our left. Here Hull's division left us." They continued on and the next day arrived at the Bruneau.[EM] McComas, too, mis-identified this river. He called it "Catherine creek or Middle river. Met a pack train and about 100 soldiers going to Salmon Falls. We found 200 soldiers camped on this creek, and also the Iowa boys & Capt., Kenneday's train. We were very glad to see them. It looked almost like home to see a face that we once seen at home in Iowa. Found them in fair spirits."[EM]

The next day, 1 September, McComas laid "by all day on this creek. The scene in camp quite a curosity. Looked up this creek from where I see three trains with soldiers encampment looks like a town. Tents are spread, women washing and cooking, children playing, men busy doing numerous things.

Droves of cattle laying around."[EM] The new train, now led by
William Carseley, was reckoned by Judson as

> about 100 strong & mostly good & brave men - among
> them Joe's old friend, Mr. Russel - the weather today is
> a trifle cooler - The new train Capt has about 40
> wagons & 100 men & some good looking women -
> They have an occasional dance & get over the road in
> good spirits At their request we all remain here another
> day & all are in hope that the train supposed to be seen
> may arrive before night - We have quite a populous
> City here of about 600 souls - 125 wagons & about 850
> animals - Dancing is going on in Capt K's train this eve
> & Jig dancing & songs in the new one.[J]

While guarding the cattle Alvin Zaring's "gun was accidentally discharged and nine buck shot passed so near my head
that I fell to the ground. In the afternoon while dragging for
fish, I was helping to hold the drag down. I found the water
was getting too deep for me as I could not swim. I turned to go
back but there was a swift undercurrent that took me down in
deep water. I sank and rose the fourth time before I was taken
out."[3]

Another train came during the night, some 18 wagons,
mostly from Denver. "They have been exempt from Indian
troubles." "They tell us that there is a large emigration coming
behind us."[J HS]

Bristol thought "a full thousand persons were camped
upon" the Bruneau River, which he called Catharine Creek.
"We staid there a week and recruited our hungry horses."
Robert Scott had been "here 8 days and there is about 1200
people here now, about 2300 head of stock in all, making quite
a city. They all have been telling of terrible hardships and
experiences. There are doctors, lawyers, preachers and many

other professional men among us, but that did not keep the Indians away. We all look alike to the hostil Indians."[RS B]

The wagon trains left the Bruneau encampment on Wednesday, 3 September. The Bristol Train must have left first as Judson was "roused at 3 o'clk & by 5 o'clk we roll out of camp comfort alone leaving it with mingled feelings of regret at the leaving & anxiety to get on."[J]

> When we get fairly on the road at the suggestion of the Capt the men shoulder their guns - take positions in the raw [*sic?*] & rear & on we go - We make by half past eleven the river about 13 miles - After a good deal of contention & cross firing we vote to remain here till morning - The train which came last into camp before last night - comes on about two hours later closely followed by Kenneddys train - The latter lost half their cattle last night by stampede but had recovered them & come on - Mr. Russel - an old acquaintance of Joe's & whom we saw several times on the Platte came along with us & is now a member of our family.[J]

Hamilton Scott and McComas both indicated they drove fifteen miles, which put them 3–4 miles northwest of Grandview, Idaho. McComas: "Camp on Snake river, found grass in the hills 2 miles from the road. Today found a skeleton near the river. Camped near the Iowa City boys and Kenneday's train."[EM]

]   Castle Creek   [

About noon the next day, the 4th, the Bristol Train reached Castle Creek. Judson described Castle Butte:

> so called from some singular looking rocks having the appearance of old dilapidated castles & other ruins -

soon Capt K.'s train arrives & Corralls near us - After
remaining an hour & a half we are ordered to hitch up
& drive on a mile or so for better grass - With rather a
bad grace (our load being nearly all on the ground &
our party scattered about) we comply & find grass
higher than our heads & Just abreast of the Castle rock
- on the other side of the corral runs the creek a small
crooked stream - behind us the open road with
Kenneddys train & a mile or more higher up the stream
the new train comes late to the creek & corralls.[J]

McComas came "to Castle Creek. Here are large hills of
burned rock that look like old ruined castles. Camped near
Kenneday's and Bristols trains."[EM]
Judson for the first time on the trip tried the first watch.
"Nothing unusual occurs during the night." The next day he
recorded, "it is said the Indians two years ago besieged a party
of 30 or 35 men on the very spot on which we were corralled &
killed all but 3 after a 3 days fight - Some report seeing nearly
a whole skeleton on the ground - I myself saw a skull &
probably could have found more by searching."[J]
Henry Judson was referring to the Utter-Van Ornum Train
of eight wagons that had camped in the same spot on Castle
Creek. On 9 September 1860, the train headed down the trail
along the Creek only a short distance before they came to a
grave. It belonged to a man from the sheep train that had
passed there a few days ahead of them. He had been buried,
and the Indians had dug him up and taken his clothing. This
was the "nearly whole skeleton" and "skull" seen by Judson.
As the Utter Train passed over the high ground west of
Castle Creek, they were first accosted by the Indians. After the
Indians failed to stampede the stock of the circled train, the
emigrants were allowed to pass on. As the train came down a
ravine onto Henderson Flat, it was ambushed. The train was
circled for defense. All through that day, the night, and until

evening of the 10th, the Utter Train battled the attacking Indians. The Indians overpowered the wagon train. Eleven men, women, and children of the 44 persons were killed here—the survivors fled down the Snake River.*

Sherlock Bristol recorded what he saw, although erroneous in the details and date:

> Pursuing our journey, we camped one night on Castle Creek. About a mile from this we came upon the ruins of the "Van Zant" [Van Ornum] train, which a year [two years] before was here ambushed and captured by the Indians. It was a sad sight—the charred remains of wagons, the bones of cattle and horses, and the skulls of murdered men and women! Some of the skulls were perforated with rifle bullets. These were scattered about, the work of these devils of the desert. I afterward fell in with one of the two who alone [Reith brothers] escaped that massacre. And the tale of horror he told was frightful. And he wept like a child, as he narrated to me how his lady love was slain there. How she stood by him night and day through all the siege and defence. How she loaded guns for him, encouraged him and brought food to him, till at last she fell at his side, perforated with balls and faint with hunger and thirst and loss of blood. I wish I could repeat her dying words to him—so brave, so sensible, so affectionate, even in death—but they are gone from me ...
>
> And we threw down the skulls and bones resolved, that if they got our skulls, they would have to pay for them! And if any of us had started out on this trip, with the soft sentiment that the white man is always to blame for these Indian troubles their minds were disabused of that false idea by this time.[B]

---

*This is described in detail in Volume II, *The Utter Disaster on the Oregon Trail*.

]   Wagon Trains North of the Snake   [

The Bristol Train started first the next day but was overtaken by the Carseley Train, "who report the meetings of two
Indians who say that a heap of wagons are passing down on the
other side of the river." The emigrants surmised that the
wagons had probably been up to Deer Lodge, in Montana, or
"Ft. Linhigh the old mormon settlement & Flowing Mill," in
Lemhi County, Idaho.[J]

The "heap of wagons" that Judson referred to could not
have been from Fort Lemhi on the Salmon River. They were
other trains, one in which 14-year-old Oliver B. Slater was in:

> After camping on Snake River four day, waiting for
> teams to come up, on the fifth day we left with a train
> of 338 wagons, eight hundred and twenty men and
> about 1400 head of stock ... There was fifty armed
> men on horses went ahead as guards and fifty more that
> brought up the rear. The teams were driven by women
> and boys so far as possible, and the men marched in
> squads of twenty each to guard the train ... Lost River
> is a stream forty feet wide and three feet deep. At this
> camp my Father died from Mountain Fever; he was
> buried by the side of the road in a coffin made of a
> wagon box. This place is ten miles southeast of where
> Arco now is.[4]

This July of 1862 Slater's train was following the Jeffrey
Cutoff. The "road that had not been traveled since 1854 and
was very dim and rocky." The emigrants had to keep

> scouts out hunting road every day. There were Indians
> on every side; they were very ugly ... we crossed the
> Lava beds to Little Wood River. Here we found 1000
> Indian warriors in camp, not a squaw or papoose among
> them. They had several hundred head of horses and

mules they had stolen off the Overland Road. The captain of the train gave orders to camp, and we pulled in about 200 yards distance from their camp. The Indians were surly and said if they had ammunition they would clean out our camp. That night there was a guard of 250 men surrounding the stock that belonged to the train, with all wagons inside the guard circle. Those Indians had lots of gold coin that they had taken from two brothers by the name of Campbell, they had murdered on Lander's cut-off near Green River.[5]

In the Boise Valley the train "tried to find a crossing at an old ford, but after having one man by the name of Curtis drowned, we gave up trying to cross there and kept down the South Side of the Boise River until we reached the Snake." It took the emigrants four days to cross the Snake River between the mouth of the Boise and that of the Owyhee. On the Malheur they "found a company of soldiers with a provision train with a supply for the emigrants."

Also, traveling north of the Snake River was the large wagon train led by the noted mountaineer, Tim Goodale. Several wagons and small trains had formed together to join the gold rush to the Warrens and Florence—the Salmon River mines. Goodale well knew the country, had an Indian wife, and got on well with the native people. Goodale warned the emigrants that they could not get their wagons to the mining area but he could take them as close to the mines as was possible.

Dunham Wright was in that large train, of some 300 wagons which crossed the Snake River ten miles above Fort Hall and followed the Jeffrey Cutoff over Camas Prairie. They traveled with "a working crew ahead, a guard on either side and a guard behind, for the Indians had on their war paint and could be seen in groups on all sides, determined we should not go on the north side of Snake river ... struck the old Oregon

Trail at the massacre grounds, where a whole train was massacred in '52. This route had not been traveled since."

Wright was referring to the 1854 attack on the Perry Train that occurred not far before the Jeffrey Cutoff rejoined the Oregon Trail. Also to the Ward Massacre that had occurred the following day, in 1854, on the Boise River near Middleton.

The Goodale Train left the Oregon Trail after crossing "the Boise river near Middleton, then making a road over the hills to the Payette, then on to the middle valley of the Weiser." Goodale had cut a new route for wagons to travel. He followed the Indian trails, taking the train up Mann Creek, through the small Thousand Spring Valley,* down Midvale Hill, and on to Cambridge, on the Weiser River. "Here it was that our 'Moses,' old Tim Goodell, was forced to acknowledge that he was lost."

Of course Goodale was not lost—he was merely at a loss as how to get wagons any closer to the mines. The gold rush traffic coming from the West going to Florence, departed from the Oregon Trail near Baker, Oregon and crossed the Snake River on the new Brownlee Ferry. The miners then followed Brownlee and Pine Creeks to the Weiser River at Cambridge.

> We remained here for ten days, grub running short and could find no way out. Finally some of our men ran across Brownlee's ferry on Snake river and Brownlee came out to find us and pilot the emigrant train by way of his ferry. But a road had to made to and from it ... Eight of our party were determined not to be disappointed in reaching Florence, the object of our

*This passed by where the author lived in 1941, and started 1st grade in the one-room Thousand Springs school. Through his research, James McGill, with local historians, has recently traced the route of the large, 1862 Goodale Wagon Train. A more direct route in Idaho, from Cambridge to Emmett, was included with the route of the Goodale Train and, incorporating the Jeffrey Cuttoff, became known as the "Goodale Road" and the "Goodale Cutoff."

destination, so they parted company with the train here and with three wagons took to the mountains.[6]

Those emigrants on the Goodale Train in joining the rush, ended up traveling by foot or by mule or horse, on to Florence. The road that the men from this train made for Brownlee rejoined the Oregon Trail at Flagstaff Hill, near Baker. The following year the gold rush to the Boise Basin shortened the route by cutting directly across the hills from Cambridge to Emmett. This new route for emigrant and miners, along with Jeffrey's Cutoff, became known as the Goodale Cutoff.

]   Wagon Trains South of the Snake Continue   [

The men from the Carseley Train also told Judson that they saw five or six other Indians at a distance. Also that last evening, the 4th, some of their party with glasses saw some 25 Indians come to the creek some miles above their encampment. The Indians were there to get their stock which was grazing there, either on Catherine or Castle Creek. "The fires we saw yesterday on the mountain we are satisfied were signals of some kind."[J]

On Friday, 5 September 1862, the wagon trains crossed Sinker Creek and then made the difficult ascent of the Sinker Creek grade. McComas: "Here we rested and watered our cattle and prospected for gold. Found from 5 to 15 grains or colors of gold in each pan. Here we had to climb the worst hill on the Oregon Road." They had to double team.[EM] The Bristol Train stopped for noon on Sinker Creek, then "immediately beginning to rise a long hard hill - We have to use lariats of old on most of the wagons & have very hard work - From the top we can see ... the two ox trains reaching from the foot of the hill far off to the east."[J]

Judson continued: "Quite a sensation was created in our camp this morning by the report of the discovery of gold in the little cold creek at the foot of the big hill we climbed yesterday - They report finding considerable color & some of our party were strongly in favor of going back & following the prospect up to the mountains."[J]

Sunday, 7 September, McComas, "Went up Current Creek prospecting." They were actually on Reynolds Creek in Owyhee County, Idaho. He "could raise the color" of gold. "Came back in the afternoon and had preaching in our corrall by Capt. Bristol the fighting Capt., of the Iowa train ... It was curious group for to be at church, the men with bowie knives and revolvers to their belts, in their shirt sleeves and buckskin pants, with one exception. One old fellow sit up as stiff as a churn dash with a starched shirt and linen coat on."[EM]

Hamilton Scott: "The trains that were with us today laid by."[HS] In outfitting his and other families, Kennedy had "laid in enough provisions to last four months, for he figured that we could make the trip in that length of time."[7] Four months had passed since the Kennedys had started out. Judson contrasted the poor families in the Kennedy Train.

> Capt K's train moved on this morning - Report says some of their Co. are living on bread & water - flour being the only provisions they have ... Capt Jacks "Happy Camp" vote to remain here all day - After breakfast a party goes to the mountain on the south about 5 miles prospecting - they find the color but no great quantity - They find some Wickeyups which they burn ... We have a service at 3 O'clk in the "Happy Camp" Mr. Walcott preaching from Roms 8th 28th - A very good sermon followed by remarks by Capt Bristol ... The audience was a good one & attentive & intelligent comprising many women & some babies - They afford a pleasing contrast to Capt K's train - the superior intelligence being clearly perceptible even in the children.[J]

On the 9th the Kennedy Train crossed the Owyhee River, near the Snake River, across from the abandoned old Fort Boise some three miles distant. The Bristol Train crossed the next day. Judson saw one lone Indian "on the other side the river - He was adorned with a red shirt & with his gun on his shoulder trudged on through the sage brush without deigning to notice us with all the stoicism & indifference of his race."[J]

"We are again in the United States - the Owyhee being the boundary line between Washn Ty & the state of Oregon - It is also the boundary line between the Snake Indians (which we shall long remember) & the Ponnacs (Bonnax) - quite an important point."[J] The Northern Paiute band in the immediate area were called "Bonnocks;" their Bannock relatives originally came from here.

On the 10th the Carseley Train also crossed the Owyhee River, where McComas and party stopped to butcher a beef. "Here one of the boys went back to get an ox that had been left behind & found it shot and its throat cut by the Indians. He started back and an Indian shot at him which hurried him to camp."[EM]

Sherlock Bristol: "Drawing near the eastern boundary of Oregon, we were overtaken by a band of prospecting miners, who had first discovered the gold mines of Idaho, but were driven off by Indians. One of their number, a Mr. Grimes from Oregon was shot down by them while engaged in digging for gold. The rest fled, leaving his body unburied, and were now en route for Auburn, for help and for supplies."[B]

This, in the unfolding Idaho gold rush, was the beginning of the rush to the Boise Basin and the upper Boise River mines. New mining towns arose, Pioneerville in October 1862, Centerville in November, and Placerville on 1 December. Idaho City, beginning as Bannock and West Bannock, became the largest city in the Pacific Northwest. The miners spread out and found even more gold—and silver!

FOURTEEN

Oregon and Gold

On 13 September 1862, Henry Judson in the Bristol Train was at Farewell Bend and heading for the Auburn mines. He noted that they were then

> 100 days from Omaha - very different from the 60 we expected to be - But we are most through & its of no use to "cry for spilted milk"... Just before starting a Packer arrives in camp from below with Tobacco & Whiskey for Sale   He gives a very good report of the mines gives us the distance as 72 miles & tells us all about the country - he has a partner on Burnt River 12 miles ahead   We uncoil about 9 oclk & follow a por- tion of K's train which starts out contrary to his wishes & causes a split in their train   Several trains & parts of trains follow as fast as they can get into the road ... 5 miles from Camp we reach & leave the old Snake river again & for "positively the last" time.[J]

Four months later, Robert Scott recounted that the Kennedy train drove eight miles and camped at noon on Burnt river.

This river got its name in 1849. The Indians massacred a train and burned the wagons and tortured the emigrants by burning them with hot irons and burning sticks. They poked the irons and sticks in their mouths when they hollered or screamed or in their eyes. They killed nearly all of that train, after that it was named Burnt River. Capt. Kennedy and the others shot in our fight with the Indians have recovered and are all right. At this place Capt. Kennedy resigned as captain of our train. Our people had become dissatisfied with him and asked him to resign, because of his overbearing attitude. All seem to be glad of his resignation. Here our train was divided. Some whom the captain had furnished with teams and a few other men went with him and camped separate from us tonight.[RS]

Hamilton Scott: "Captain Kennedy resigned this morning and the company is well pleased because he did. ... We understand that we have been in Oregon for forty-five miles but we are sixty-five miles from settlement yet. The first settlement is on Powder River. They are gold miners."[HS] More than one wagon train was breaking apart. The next day Evans McComas in the William Jack or William Carseley Train:

We are just 4 months from home today and 4 months it has been too of dust, hard work & hard fare. We drove 5 miles to Burnt River and encamped in the long dreaded Burnt River Canyon near a pile of skulls of a train that had been massacre in '52 here. After we had come over 400 miles together to come through this canyon united our Capt., resigned and we are now going it every fellow for him self. I traded my shot gun for a double barreled rifle.[EM]

And Judson in the Bristol Train, that day mentioned that J.K. Root for the third or fourth time had seceded from the train, being particularly down upon Judson and Captain Bristol.

> Hurst the elder has also seceeded on acct of the train taking him in hand for misusing his young brother - instituting a trial to adjust financial differences between them & bringing about a settlement to the satisfaction of the younger Hurst - They joined K's train & now that it is split they hardly know to what they belong ... We have a report that a party of 30 men are successfully working claims on Brick creek 15 miles from the road - It may be true - This country should be good for something - A fellow came ahead of his team several miles yesterday to overtake friends ahead & was robbed by four Indians of everything he had which they wanted - He was unarmed & twas very little they got.[J]

So, Monday, 15 September, McComas: "Everybody for themselves this morning. Some started at daylight and some when they got ready. Kenneday's train ahead of us. Bristol's in the rear."[EM] As for the Scotts, "We have now twenty-one in our company. We have elected Mr. Hall as our Captain."[HS] Judson met three small parties of packers with horses going through to Salt Lake. One had three Indians in their employ as drivers.[J]

Going up Burnt River, Sherlock Bristol "met a band of three hundred horses, driven at headlong speed by some Indians. We were in a defile, and I demanded what they were doing with them. One of them replied, 'Salt Lake!' 'Salt Lake!' This was plausible, and we let them pass. The next day we found they had all been raided from the miners at Auburn."[B]

On the 17th, the Bristol Train was on the road being marshaled by W.G. Ives as Captain Bristol with "Jack" Hank Humphrey had gone up the little stream on our right to ascertain the cause of disturbance in the water - Before we leave camp a report is current that a lot of mining tools & provisions have been discovered a short distance up the creek - 3 miles from the creek we meet Mr. Culbertson an acquaintance of some of our party with 4 others & 3 Pack horses - who are just from Powder River & are prospecting this country   They report Powder River as good or even better than we have before heard it - also that 50 men are mining on the little stream before mentioned & 100 men on the head waters of Powder & Brunt Rivers about 50 miles to the North West of us - They tell us also that the 3 parties we met with horses had stolen them from Ranchers on Powder River - Would that we had known it & intercepted them ... We finally bring up at the Spring the last watering place this side of Powder River 18 miles distant - Here we find fragments of Kenneddys & Capt Jacks trains they being broken all to pieces.[J]

The next day the Bristol camp was on the west side of Powder river

just below the ford in grass higher than ones head - The ford is graced by a Ranche ... well supplied with good Beef - It is the first thing in the shape of a house we have seen since long before we left the Cut Off [at South Pass] - Here are camps on all sides - some cutting hay - some ranching cattle & horses - some preparing to plant out - prospecting ... The train comes in, in pieces but all get together in a tolerable corral - Hank starts for Auburn 10 miles distant on his mule ... After Supper our Capt calls a meeting of the train & in a very neat & pretty speech - congratulates the train on their safe arrival in the "happy land of Canaan" - compliments them for general good behavior - observance of the Sabbath etc. Expresses his opinion that tis the first whole train as well as most intelligent & refined that has or will cross the plains this season ... & as they had no further use for a Capt - tendered his resignation & disbanded his train.[J]

Mr. Henley in behalf of the Iowa City party thanked Captain Bristol for forbearance for services kindly rendered. Mr. Cassady, the wounded man, returned thanks to the whole Company for kindness and attention. A resolution was unanimously adopted profusely thanking Sherlock Bristol for the train having safely and with unusual, good success performed the long, tedious and perilous journey across the plains from the Missouri river to the State of Oregon. Judson continued in his detailed reporting[J]

Resolved
That in Capt Bristol-we have found a brave-faithful-efficient & willing commander - A social - agreeable & instinctive companion - an excellent teacher & a faithful & true friend

Resolved
That we hereby tender him our heartfelt thanks for the abundant services so freely & ably rendered & that in taking leave of him as our Chief we still hope to retain him as our friend.[J]

"From this last encampment we gradually separated and went our several ways, the most of us to meet no more ... the attachment then formed to those companions in tribulation" remained fresh and strong. It was a great pleasure to Bristol to "meet several of them during a subsequent residence of nearly two years in Idaho."[B]

Also on the 18th Evans McComas started early. After going eight miles, came to where the emigrants separate,

> those going to the mines turn to the left. Those going to the Willammett and Wallah Wallah Valleys to the right. Here was a grand division. Some men who had come togather from the States, one would want to go on and the other to the mines. Things were thrown around in all shapes. Some were going through with packs, some without. Here was a general shaking of hands and bidding good bye. The people of the train had come so far and traveled so long and passed through danger togather over such a long and toilsome jounrney that they had become fast friends. Our team turned for Auburn.[EM]

]   Auburn   [

Also on 18 September, Hamilton Scott arrived "where the roads part, one leading to Fort Walla Walla and the other to Powder River gold mines at Auburn, Oregon. I, with a number of others took the latter road. Camped on Powder River ten miles from Auburn."[HS] Robert Scott:

> Several trains left our main train and went for Auburn. Some of us went on horseback to get mail then returned. Got into Auburn, a mining town about noon, just in time to see them hang a man for poisoning his partner. He had his trial and did not seem to be worried. They asked him if he had anything to say. He said he forgave all but two men who swore to lies. Then put his hand in his pocket and gave his interpreter his money (he was an Italian), his watch to the minister who was on the scaffold to pray for him. Then the sheriff pulled the cap over his face, then stepped back

and pulled the trap and he dropped, broke his neck and gave a few kicks and that was the last of him. Friday the 13th was his unlucky day. Auburn is like other mining towns, the toughest places in the world. At this same time they had a gambler waiting trial for killing two men. They brought him out for trial, out in the open, near the gallows where the Italian was hanged. The sheriff was taking him through the crowd, when up rode a man on a horse and threw his rope over the prisoners head. Then put spurs to his horse and dragged him off down a street full of stumps and rocks to a tree and hung him up on a limb, but he was dead before he got to the tree. We thought this was the toughest place in the world. We went to the post office and got some mail, then rode our horses back to the train on Burnt River.[RS]

Further history of Auburn was found in the *Commonwealth Review*, March, 1939:

The founding of Auburn was an indirect result of an early search for the fabled "Blue Bucket" diggings, lost in 1845. A group of prospectors in northeastern Oregon were on their way back to Portland in October, 1861, after an unsuccessful search for the Blue Bucket mine. One of the party, Henry Griffin, found good placer prospects in what became known as Griffin's Gulch. The reports were good enough to start a rush. Searches were made in neighboring canyons, and new discoveries located. The town of Auburn was laid out on the flat at the junction of Blue Canyon and Freezeout Gulch. Auburn became the center of a lively mining district favored with the usual colorful names, Jackass Gulch, Five-bit Gulch, Forty-nine Gulch, and Hogem.[EM]

William Purvine wrote a letter to the editor of the *Salem Oregon Statesman*, "To day a considerable number of immigrants have arrived here from the Western States and Denver City, C.T. Among them are several wounded men, who have escaped from the massacres along Snake river. I am permitted to take from the memorandum of Mr. V.D. Johnson, of Denver, the following ..." Purvine then described the attack east of Fort Hall where five miners from Denver were killed and two wounded. He also listed those killed and wounded in the "skirmish" with the Indians at Massacre Rocks. He ended his letter, "To day a part of our company set out for Boise river. The others follow soon. We have in all about 70 men."[1]

So, some miners were leaving Auburn for the Boise Basin just as the emigrants were arriving. On the 19th McComas also went to Auburn, "found it a town of about 200 houses. Saw a man hung. Miners at work."[EM] McComas' arrival in Auburn coincided with the hanging of Lucien Gamier, executed, legally, for the strychnine poisoning of his partner. According to a contemporary newspaper account, this was "the first execution for murder in this camp," and followed a two-day trial conducted with "decorum and dignity." Two months later, McComas noted the lynching, in Auburn, of "Spanish Tom," an affair described in indignant detail by the *Oregonian* correspondent.[EM]

The same day that McComas went to Auburn, Judson, after breakfast,

> many left camp for Auburn on foot leaving the train to move up the river about 8 miles to grass - I went with the party on foot & in a little over 3 hours walk we reach the town a flourishing mining town of about 200 log houses & more all the time being built - Many families still occupy their tents or a bower temporarily - We were just too late by only a few minutes to see a frenchman hung for poisoning his companions one of

whom died - He was tried in judge Lynch's court by a jury - convicted & was hanging when we arrived - There were probably 1000 people assembled to witness the execution - I found the town flourishing & lively - nearly every conceivable branch of business doing something - I found Stutsman & Bayles of the Bluffs - McLaughlin & family & the dark Barber Geo. from Omaha & learned with great regret that Mike Murphy has left here only yesterday for Boisee river prospecting.[J]

Judson returned to the wagons and the next morning

The camp is late astir - No one orders the stock turned out - no one rouses the camp to prepare breakfast for an early start - One at a time as inclination prompts them they appear - All good natured & at peace with everybody - No stories to be heard from the guard of the stump or rock which they had watched so closely strongly suspecting 'Twas an Indian' None yawning & grumbling for loss of rest - but all seem at home & enjoying what they are justly entitled to - a good rest with a sense of relief & a feeling that the terrible journey is at an end - After breakfast the large family dissolves - Joe [Sprott] & John [Hileman] divide in a very few minutes their effect.[J]

On the 19th also, the Scott brothers "are now in Auburn, the long sought gold field we have longed for. Here we found some men working, but could not do much work because of water. It takes lots of water to work mines, so we set to work and built a good brush house to stay in. There are 5 of us messing together here. Geo. Farbrush, Lewis Beck, Ham Scott, Wilson Scott and Myself, Robert Scott."[RS]

By the fall of 1862 Auburn and vicinity had probably passed the summit of prosperity, certainly of
opportunity. Water, a necessary ingredient of placer
mining, was particularly scarce in winter. Inflated
reports from the Boise mines were beginning to attract
miners from the Powder River diggings. A.J. Grover,
dealer in hardware, wrote to Edwin Beebe of Portland,
in December, 1862, "Auburn is very dull at the
present. I suppose that fully half the male population
has left here for Boise, and the balance would if they
had the means ... There is 150 odd families here who
crossed the plains this season. Many of them are very
poor. I can't see how some of them will get through
the winter ... We will have a ball in Auburn on
[Christmas] ... The girls here are not very pretty, but
kind ... Many of the boys are marrying—I think only
for the winter, as they are so very easy to suit."[EM]

Three days after the Scott brothers had arrived in Auburn,
they "looked around and find but few men working because of
not enough water. Since mining takes a lot of water, we can't
do much until the snow begins to thaw in the spring. Some we
found are only making a living, and others doing well. The
men who are here and acquainted can get work we find. We
will have to go to—we know not where?"[RS]

A week later they packed their horses and "started out and
kept going, looking for a place to winter and work, and landed
here, 300 miles from Auburn" at Walla Walla, Washington
Ter. That was where Robert C. Scott wrote his account of the
journey, dated 12 January 1863.[RS]

The rest of the Kennedy Train continued on to Walla
Walla. It "passed through La Grande, Oregon which had only
a few houses." On 27 September 1862 they struck their "last
camp six miles southeast of Walla Walla on Cotton Wood

Creek. Instead of being four months on the road we were six months."[2]

Captain Medorem Crawford's expedition escorting the last of the emigrant wagons arrived at the Powder River crossing on 2 October. After passing Fort Hall he had found many of the emigrant "teams so weak that they could not travel over ten miles per day others being able to proceed faster; and in order to give protection to all, I divided my company, placing the advance party in charge of my principal assistant, Mr. Le Roy Crawford, while I remained with the rear and weaker party." From then on their journey was extremely slow.[3]

Many of the emigrants were short of provisions, which the government escort had to supply. Some emigrants "had difficulties among themselves" which Crawford had to settle. "Most of the emigrants exhibited a proper appreciation of the objects of the expedition, and received very thankfully the aid and benefits bestowed upon them," by the government. "From the hostile disposition thus manifested by the Indians towards the emigrants, it is safe to conclude that the later and weaker parties would have been entirely cut off had it not been for the protection afforded them by the government."[4]

The large number of wagon trains that traveled ahead of the escort "had cut up the road to such an extent that the dust was very deep and its alkaline properties fatal to cattle." There were over forty head of dead cattle along the sixteen miles between the Owyhee and Malheur Rivers. The proportion was nearly as great at other points along the Snake River.

From his best information Crawford estimated that "the emigration to Oregon and Washington this year at 10,000 souls, about two-fifths of whom I think crossed Snake River at the Fort Hall Ferry ... The recent discoveries of gold on Boise River will doubtless attract large parties from the States next season and a road on the north side, will be very necessary."[5]

The next year, 1863, Medorem Crawford did the same thing, escorting emigrant trains overland to the Pacific

Northwest, again as an Army captain. From 1864 to 1869 he was collector of internal revenue for the state of Oregon, and from 1871 to 1875 he served as appraiser of customs. Crawford died in 1891.

In Auburn, Evans McComas stayed with the Iowa City boys and bought two town lots to build their cabins on. He went for supplies and returned "to Auburn November 11th and found the folks all well. George was working at 2.50 per day. The town which started in the spring now contains as many as 1000 houses and some 60 stores. A Spaniard killed two men here with a knife. The miners took him and drug him down town by the heels and then hung him. A greaser shot into the crowd and wounded 3 men. The miners shot him. We traded for the one half of two claims on freeze out gulch and now are working them."[EM]

Auburn reached its peak of prosperity in 1863 with an estimated population of 6,000. By December 1864 it was "fast going to decay" with its population estimated at around 250. The County seat was moved to Baker in 1868. "In 1945 nothing remained to mark the site of Auburn."[6]

McComas left Auburn and joined Sherlock Bristol in a subsequent rush to Idaho City.[7] Evans S.McComas was born in Adams County, Ohio, 23 January 1839. He died at Wallowa, Oregon, 4 September 1911.[EM] Sherlock Bristol

> began at once to prospect the hills and valleys for mining claims. But while I could find "the color" or small particles of gold almost anywhere over a large section of country, there were few places where it was concentrated in paying quantities.
>
> The news from Idaho being favorable, Messrs. Bainan and Walcott, McComb [McComas?]and myself formed a company, sold our cabin and all we could spare and invested in a couple of yoke of oxen, a wagon and supplies, and started off for the new mining placer.

It was midwinter and bitterly cold, and much we suffered before we reached the end of our journey, 300 miles distant."[B]

Bristol and the other miners "located at Placerville, and at once commenced sawing our lumber by hand. We had brought along a saw from Auburn for that purpose." His partners "being well settled for the winter in a fair business of sawing lumber," Bristol struck out for himself. "Went over to Mores Creek (now Idaho City) and formed a partnership with one William Henry from Illinois."[B]

"In March of '63" Dunham Wright "whipsawed the lumber that built the first lumber house in Idaho City, for James Pinney."[8]

Four months later, in July, a new Army post was established: on the Boise River, on the Oregon Trail, and as close to the Boise mines as possible. Boise City immediately sprang up by this new "Fort Boise." The Army built a bridge across the Boise River (Capital Blvd) and Oregon Trail traffic from then on crossed the Boise there.

Some emigrants now followed along the north side of the Boise to its mouth where a ferry was again established to cross the Snake. Midway down this route, Middletown grew up—soon shortened to Middleton. Much of the traffic went cross country to the northwest, staying on the Idaho side to cross the Snake River on the Washoe Ferry (between the mouths of the Malheur and the Payette) and Olds Ferry (at Farewell Bend). One mile above where it empties into the Snake a bridge was built over the Weiser River—the town of Weiser Bridge soon grew there. In December 1863, in the midst of the Civil War and the Idaho Gold Rush, a new US Territory was created—Idaho!

ALMO IDAHO
DEDICATED TO THE MEMORY
OF THOSE WHO LOST THEIR LIVES IN A MOST
HORRIBLE INDIAN MASSACRE 1861.
THREE HUNDRED IMMIGRANTS WEST BOUND
ONLY FIVE ESCAPED.
ERECTED BY S & D OF IDAHO PIONEERS
1938

The fictional Almo Massacre Monument.

Photo by Author, Almo, ID, 2 April 2008.

Appendix I

Almo Massacre Legend

After 1860, Pocatello's Shoshoni band, who occupied City of Rocks and other nearby valleys, resisted emigrant traffic through that area. Idaho's expanding gold rush brought ever more problems, along with devastating military campaigns. "Shoshoni resentment to pressure from miners—and from extensive armed attacks—became much more intense."[1]

A new dimension of Shoshoni tribal legends came about and eventually gained attention from other people as well. "Although its geographical setting is close to Almo and City of Rocks, it entered Idaho historical literature from North Ogden, Utah."

The legend included elements of actual attacks on emigrant trains, in the year before and the year after this fictional Almo massacre was to have occurred. In 1860 when within five miles of City of Rocks, near the junction with the Salt Lake road, a twenty-member wagon train was attacked by about sixty Indians. Two days later the wagons were moved to a new location, but on this third night the emigrants had to abandon their wagons and flee.* In 1862 Jane Gould mentioned the Walker train digging trenches, beginning near Almo and for several nights thereafter

---

*See Volume II, *The Utter Disaster On The Oregon Trail*, Appendix I, "Wagon Train Taken at City of Rocks, 1860," and Appendix IV, "1861 Attack on the Harriman Train."

until through the City of Rocks and into Nevada, "dug trenches again. Dug a deep hole on one of the hills for the pickets to stand in."[G]

> William Edward Johnston (who always was known as Edward) came to Utah in 1852 with his family when he was only five years old. When he grew up in North Ogden, he became a close friend of some local Shoshoni and Ute Indians. Eventually he learned both languages. He also heard fascinating accounts of clashes between Pocatello's band and emigrant parties near Almo. In 1872, he toured Almo Valley, where he noticed traces of campground circles along with remnants of wagons and emigrant equipment.[2]

Eventually Johnston homesteaded in the Almo Valley in 1887. One of his North Ogden informants, Winecus, provided Johnston a "Shoshoni legendary account of a battle to explain those Almo relics." Winecus had told that "some 3,000 Shoshoni and Ute warriors assembled quietly near Almo, where they wiped out a party of some 300 emigrants from Missouri, whom they dumped into a couple of wells before they departed quietly to go on about their business. Some later reports of that affair raised emigrant losses to more than 340."[3]

Winecus' tale countered a widely accepted emigrant tendency to pass off Shoshoni peoples as poor, incapable diggers. Other accounts embellished Winecus' lore. His "version brought a distinctive Indian aspect to a kind of folklore that has characterized emigrant traditions" of Indian hazards. In the tale, contained in the August 1970 *100 Years of Progress Edition* of the Burley *South Idaho Press*, "The only records rest in the memory of old people who lived at that time or in the accounts handed down from parent to child."[4]

Writer Says Almo Massacre Was Most Important Indian Disaster in Idaho
By CHARLES SHIRLEY WALGAMOTT
(submitted by Etta Taylor, of Almo, Idaho)

The Battle of Almo Creek was the most important Indian disaster in the history of Idaho. It happened in Cassia County with five survivors out of 300 white men.

Undoubtedly the greatest Indian disaster that ever occurred in the Territory of Idaho and probably the entire Northwest, when we consider the number slain, was the massacre of Almo Creek in 1861.

Out of some 300 persons, men, women and children, only five—three men and two women—were known to have escaped the cruel death administered to them by the overwhelming band of Indians that had congregated for days in such great numbers that they were enabled to hold in siege a train of emigrants who were well-organized, well-armed and provisioned, and well-equipped with fine stock drawing more than 60 wagons.

Despite the magnitude of this onslaught very little, if anything, has been written in regard to it. The only records rest in the memory of old people who lived at that time or in the accounts handed down from parent to child.

The writer, Charles Shirley Walgamott, visited the battleground in 1875. Evidence of the conflict was marked plainly by trenches thrown up under each wagon as they were arranged in circles. Accompanying the party was an old trapper who gave a detailed account of the tragedy. In putting this story together Charles Walgamott took considerable pains to verify what he saw and heard on the subject.

The best informer was Mr. William E. Johnston who with his wife spent the latter part of his life in Twin Falls. They were 14 and 12 years of age, respectively, at the time of the massacre and were living in the settlement of North Ogden. The impressions made on their young minds were stamped clearly. They remembered the first man and woman who escaped from the besieged train and made their way to the settlement of Brigham City, Utah, where a rescue party was dispatched to the scene. On their way they found, on Raft River, two women, one man, and a baby who had escaped and for several days had existed on rosebuds as their only food. They remembered that the Indians returned and passed through the settlement displaying the scalps of their victims attached to the manes and bridles of their ponies. They recalled seeing a North Ogden blacksmith and a party going to salvage the iron from the burned wagons.

In 1872, 11 years later, Mr. Johnston visited the battlefield and in 1887 the Johnston family moved to Almo Creek securing land that partially covered the battlefield which still bore evidence of the hard-fought battle. In leveling and plowing the ground for alfalfa. Mr. Johnston uncovered numerous old guns and pistols.

Mr. Johnston spoke the Shoshoni language well enough to be understood and from an Indian he was able to get the Indian version of the massacre which is, in part, incorporated in the following story:

THE INDIAN ACCOUNT.

In the spring of 1861 an emigrant train left the Missouri River bound for California. It was equipped as nearly as possible with everything necessary to make safe the trip through an unsettled country infested with Indians, the train consisted of more than 60 wagons and some 300 souls. Nothing is known of the early part of their trip until they reached the Western Plains where they were harassed by Indians whom they were able to keep at bay through their well-organized camp, their driving management, and their equipment of arms.

This gave then added courage and they looked on the Indians, who at first were small in numbers, with indifference and sometimes they took shots at them at long range to keep them away. which angered the Indians. This. together with the natural antipathy which they felt for the white man. coupled with the desire to destroy the train and possess its belongings, caused a general uprising of the numerous Indians whose habitats were adjacent to the Oregon Trail.

Indian runners were sent out and smoke signals were sent up. The place of concentration was to be Indian Grove, some four or five miles south of Almo Creek. According to the Indians' account there was assembled here the largest number of hostile Indians ever known in these parts. Here they provisioned their camp with game meat, which was plentiful, and waited for the condemned train.

The emigrants traveled over the Oregon Trail until they crossed Raft River, where their guide headed them south over the Sublett cut-off to the California trail. They traveled peacefully for three short days without sighting Indians, and then camped for the night on Almo Creek, so named by the Indians signifying "plenty water," where now nestles the peaceful town of Almo. Here they took their usual precautions, made a corral of their wagons, placed strong guards over their stock, and slept peacefully, not knowing that an overwhelming band of blood thirsty Indians were looking down at them from Indian Grove, a large elevated mountain bench finely-timbered. which even today retains its name.

The outpost of the Indians watched with impatience the emigrants light their morning fire inside their wagon enclosure; watched the herdsmen drive their stock to camp to be harnessed for the day's journey; and saw the line of defense being broken; each wagon falling into its alloted position in almost military precision. The Indians were in readiness. They were about to attack a foe much superior in arms and ammunition, The Indians had a few guns and small quantities of ammunition, but they depended on their greater numbers, their bows and arrows and their well-planned mode of attack.

They allowed the train, as it moved slowly southward from Almo Creek, to proceed until its rear wagon was some distance from the creek. Suddenly a prearranged signal was given by the Indian lookout, and Indians in great numbers emerged from their places of concealment where they had lurked in silence and secrecy. They completely surrounded and surprised emigrants who immediately gave orders for all wagons to be corraled with all stock inside the enclosure. This was accomplished in site of the hair-raising yells of the bloodthirsty Indians who knew they had committed the first act of their contemplated tragedy. They had the emigrant train cut off from water and the siege began. It was not to be a fight where man was given for man, but was fought in Indian fashion, each Indian protecting himself, reserving his ammunition, keeping the train in siege until the emigrants had exhausted their ammunition and were famished for water. A large portion of the Indians secretly retired to their camps in Indian Grove leaving only enough of their tribesmen to hold the siege and from protected points of vantage picked off with arrows or guns any emigrant that attempted to escape or get water. In relays, the Indians, day and night harassed the whites with arrows, guns and firebrands shot into the wagons and otherwise terrorized them by yells, which were joined in by the entire Indian war parties. This was intended to impress on the minds of the confused emigrants the overwhelming majority of Indians.

DESPERATE CONDITION

The emigrants realized their condition, and under each wagon a trench was dug with the dirt thrown to the outside. The digging of a well was started in hopes of getting water. This work was carried on feverishly until it proved disappointing. Men who attempted to bring water from the creek were shot down.

Occasionally shots from the Indians killed or badly wounded some white man, woman, or child which threw the members of the besieged party into greater excitement and grief. The excitement grew intense as panic-stricken horses in their struggles broke their fastenings and ran frantically around the enclosure while others in their attempts to break loose were snorting, rearing, and trampling the earth from which rose great columns of dust through which frantic women and children darted hither and thither in their aimless attempt for relief. This, with constant yelling of the Indians and howling of their dogs made a scene too wild and awful to contemplate.

On the third day the stock was ordered turned from the enclosure. As they hastened for water they were taken into the possession of the Indians. Little by little the fighting force of the train was reduced and the remainder contemplated the inevitable.

It was on the fourth night that the guide employed by the wagon train gave up all hopes and planned his escape. He was accompanied by a young woman who had displayed great courage and marksmanship. Under the protection of darkness they crawled through the sagebrush, making their way to the mountains. After hours and hours of travel, they found their way to the settlement of Brigham City, Utah. In the after part of the same night one man and two women, one with a nursing baby, secretly stole from the doomed camp, crawling for miles on their hands and knees. The mother of the child in her anguish and endeavor to keep in company with the others as they crawled through the brush, was compelled to take the garments of the child in her teeth and carry it in that manner.

They were successful in making their escape, reaching a point on Raft River which was afterwards known as the E. Y. Ranch, where they lived on rosebuds and roots until found by a rescue party from Brigham City, who sent them on to the settlement and then proceeded to the battleground of Almo Creek to find the entire party slain and the wagons burned. The bodies of the unfortunate people were buried in the well which they had dug.

The battleground was visited in 1875. Evidence of the conflict was marked plainly by trenches thrown up under each wagon as they were arranged in circles.[5]

Another version of the fictional Almo Massacre surfaced a little later. In the foregoing account the battleground was visited in 1875 and evidence of the conflict was plainly marked by trenches thrown up under each of the circles wagons. In 1883 John Peters visited a Mr. Durfee who took Peters to the "scene of the conflict and told him of the scene he and two companions, Mr. Seldon Cutler and Mr. Ezra Barnard, encountered when they went to bury the dead." The following account does not explain how Mr. Durfee come to be at Almo, both in 1861 and twenty-two years later in 1883.[6]

The Massacre at the City of Rocks
Taken from an address by John D. Peters; July 26, 1928

The massacre at the City of Rocks is one of the cruelest on record. It occurred during the summer of 1861. A party of wealthy Eastern emigrants—forty in number—were traveling enroute to California over the old Oregon Trail. In its possession was a large herd of cattle which the company drove—as was the custom in early emigration—in advance of its own progress, the wagon train following the herd at a short distance. Herein lay the cause of the massacre.

Arriving at a point along the Oregon Trail somewhere in the vicinity of the present site of American Falls, the party left the trail in favor of what was known as the Southern cut-off. This latter course passed down through the northern part of Box Elder County, through Nevada and over the route followed by the equally ill fated Donner party in 1846.

When the company arrived at a point along their line of march adjacent with the present site of Almo, Idaho, they set up what, unwittingly, was to be their last camp on the banks of what was then known as Durfee's creek. This creek has since become better known as Almo creek.

Almo is situated to the east of a high bluff. Just back of this bluff is a beautiful cove valley and west of the valley is a high mountain lookout from which the Indians could view vast sweeps of the Idaho country. It is probable that the Indians caught sight of the wagon train several days before it reached the unfortunate camp at Almo, or Durfee's creek, and had their plans well laid by the time the camp was made.

As the emigrants were camped at Durfee's creek, the renegade Chief Pocatello and his band were camped only a half mile away. At nine o'clock in the morning the emigrants broke camp and strung their cattle out ahead of them as was their usual practice. The wagon had barely pulled out of the ill fated camp when the Indians rushed from a small ravine, cutting the emigrants from their cattle and the herders and forcing them back into a corral formation for self defense.

Behind their fortifications in the corral the emigrants defended themselves through three nights of almost constant fighting. They had no water which must have intensified them suffering immensely. A trench was dug in which the women and children sought safety and this was probably a mistake as evidenced by the tales of torture told by three members of the party who made good their escape. The Indians were numerous and had determined leadership. They stayed with the fight, employing those tactics which would tell most heavily on their opponents with a minimum of loss to themselves.

The three fortunate enough to escape massacre, a man and two women, made their way to Raft River. Following the stream through the narrows they traveled in a southeasterly direction from the head of Raft River valley over the south pass of the Black Pine valley into Curlew valley and across the Promontory into the Bear River valley and eventually found their way to a herd house owned jointly by George Reeder and George Parsons. There they were discovered and brought across the river to the home of Bishop Alvin Nichols where they stayed for some time.[7]

Appendix II

Legend of Bigfoot, Chief Nampuh

Prior to white settlement of Idaho and eastern Oregon, Shoshoni and Northern Paiutes (indiscriminately called Snake Indians) traveled over vast areas in search of food. One of their leaders was Howluck, a noted chief, who ranged with his band from the Owyhees and the Boise and Weiser Valleys to the Deschutes River in Oregon. In 1860, Howluck had a hundred Snake Indians on Klamath Lake, where his band menaced wagon trains coming from California.

After 1860, the gold rush into eastern Oregon and southern Idaho stirred up the Shoshoni and Northern Paiute. They resisted with raids and outright warfare against the white intruders. Among the most energetic Indian leaders to oppose the whites was Howluck, "a considerable chief of the Snake Indians," who at that time operated mainly around Canyon City, Oregon. Four years of hostilities followed a 24 June 1864 attack in that area.

> Howluck's associates were scattered from the upper Weiser and the Owyhee country westward into Oregon in a region where the army generally could not find them; operations proceeded only with great difficulty in the campaigns of the resulting Snake War.[1]

Howluck (Oualuck, or Oulux), who had fought a well-known mountaineer named Reid in a personal encounter, was a large, tall man distinguished mostly for his oversize foot, measuring 14 3/4 inches. He was noted for his stamina and prowess.

"Namb" is a Shoshone word that means "moccasin." A Shoshoni word for foot is pronounced "nambe" or "nambuh." The Indians would "stuff their moccasins, during cold weather, with sage brush leaves. This would enlarge to unusual size, the tracks of Indians wearing such stuffed moccasins." "Nampa" may be an Indian word, or an anglicized word for a term used by the Indians. There is no "doubt that the original root was a Shoshone word, and the meaning is either moccasin or footprint." Nampa primarily means "footprints" as the "imprint of the moccasin in the sand or earth," also "implying the moccasin or shoe."[2]

One can see how the term "Nampuh" was sometimes used to mean "Over-sized Moccasin" or Bigfoot. As for Howluck, "By 1866 the whites (generally unaware of any Indian name for their adversary) were calling him Bigfoot."

More than a year went by before Bigfoot with his band of sixty-one Indians was captured in eastern Oregon by a military force and an independent party of Willow Creek miners early in June, 1868. By that time, one of his associated bands had been wiped out on May 26 by an expedition from Camp Lyon, and another was out of reach on the upper Weiser. Bigfoot and his people were tired of their four year war and wanted to quit. But the Weiser band, still hostile, was not inclined to give up the advantage of terrorizing the settlers with "Bigfoot" tracks simply because Bigfoot had decided to quit the fight.[3]

The Weiser band used huge stuffed moccasins to make menacing footprints during the Army's operations against them on the Salmon in July and August, 1868. Also, the Weiser Indians may have been directing their threat against the Nez Perce. There was a Nez Perce belief that some ten years before the 1877 Nez Perce War the Bannocks were trying to scare the Nez Perce by making oversized footprints. There was a Nez Perce saying that "Even little Bannocks have big feet." In November 1869, Bigfoot finally settled on an Oregon reservation.

> There he still was noted for his ability to run down and capture jack rabbits equipped only with his cane, "incredible as it may seem, when the fleetness of these animals is considered. He would actually run out to them and knock them down with the cane."[4]

]   Bigfoot, the Legend   [

Ten years after the end of the Snake War in 1868, in which Howluck, the real Bigfoot, was a leading figure, a legend had grown up in the Northwest. The legend of Bigfoot, that first appeared in the *Idaho Statesman* on 14 and 16 November 1878, was also printed six years later in Wallace W. Elliott's 1884 *History of Idaho Territory*. "By then, Bigfoot, the legendary half-breed, was turned into a man quite different from Howluck, the real Indian with big feet ... an extra-ordinary specimen of Snake Indian."[5] In introducing "The Noted Indian, Bigfoot," Elliott remarked on the plausibility of the tale:

> Mr. Wm. T. Anderson, of Fisherman's Cove, Humboldt County, California, a former resident of Idaho, sent to the Idaho Statesman, of November, 1878, the

following account of the killing of the noted Indian Bigfoot. This Indian is remembered by many of the old settlers of Idaho. The story has all the marks of strict truthfulness. John W. Wheeler, the hero of the story, was mixed up in the attempt to rob the stage in the Blue Mountains in the autumn of 1868, and was sentenced, with several others, to ten years' imprisonment in the Oregon penitentiary. He served his term out minus the few months allowed him as credits for good behavior, and was discharged from the prison during 1877, and went to California, where it was afterward learned he committed suicide.[6]

Elliott's information on John Wheeler was correct. Four articles in the Idaho Tri-Weekly Statesman in the Spring of 1880 contained this information, although the middle initial was different. On 22 June it was reported that John F. Wheeler was "the first United States Deputy Marshall of Idaho." Two days later this fact was corrected. The confusion came from this "Slayer of Bigfoot" having helped in making some arrests of pretty desperate characters. Wheeler was then a hard-working blacksmith in Idaho City and "behaved himself in good shape." He then joined a party of road agents led by his brother-in-law, Dr. Lebur. They were suspected of robbing Welch and John Ramsey on Wood River in 1868 and Wheeler was probably the man that killed Welch. Wheeler was shadowed, and was detected and captured in the Blue Mountain stage robbery a short time later. He was convicted, sentenced to ten years imprisonment, and released from the Oregon penitentiary 17 February 1877.[7]

In many respects Wheeler was a remarkable man. "He possessed physical courage above most men; and his courage and skill with firearms made him prominent among the turbulent spirits who flocked to Idaho at an early day."[8] He told friends and relatives stories about an Indian chief in Idaho named Bigfoot.

There seems to be no record of "Wm. T. Anderson, of Fisherman's Cove, Humboldt County, California," who supposedly submitted the tale of Bigfoot to the Statesman in November 1878. This followed Wheeler's release from prison by a few months, and he left quite a record. He moved to California and served a term in that state's prison, at San Quentin. Following his release he became a dentist there in Mendicino County. In the Fall of 1879 he was arrested with other outlaws whom he led, for murdering a young man while robbing a stage. At Ukiah, on 14 May 1880, Wheeler was sentenced to hang on 2 July. He took poison the night before the scheduled hanging and died.[9]

Wheeler was well known in Idaho. With his notoriety he evidently used a pseudonym in promoting this fantastic tale to enhance his image. It mainly included "Northwestern bad men, for whom Bigfoot seems to have become something of a folk hero: the tale, in fact, seems to have evolved among stage robbers imprisoned in Oregon." The Starr Wilkinson of the legend may have existed in Oklahoma, but there is no historical evidence of his existence in Idaho.[10]

The following legend of Bigfoot was reprinted a number of times, in newspapers and dime novels. In the telling the legend took several forms. In the *Real West* magazine, January 1963, the Chief Bigfoot story was rather different from Wheeler's account.* The tale in *True* magazine, September 1957, had the settlers calling Bigfoot, "Chief Namp-puh."[11]

---

*Although raised in Western Idaho, the Author did not learn of the Legend of Bigfoot until reading it in 1958 in the *Bluebook* magazine (while in AF Navigator training at Waco, Texas).

EARLY DAYS IN IDAHO

THE BIGFOOTED FIEND.

A Thrilling Account of the Career
of the Notorious Indian Bigfoot,
and the hand to hand conflict
between him and his
slayer, J. W. Wheeler.

How and when the Terror of
Idaho was Killed.

BY AN EYE-WITNESS OF THE SCENE.

The following narrative will no doubt be interesting to many of the old pioneers of Idaho, who may have had dear relatives or friends murdered and scalped by the red-handed savages that once infested Idaho Territory to such an extent that the daring and hardy miner was not safe in wandering from his tent, or the teamster from his wagon, without his trusty rifle and revolver in hand. Whole trains of emigrants—composed of men, women, and children—were slaughtered without mercy, the bones of many of whom were left bleaching on the Boise and Snake Rivers, testifying to the hatred of the Snake Indians to the whites.

The leader, and the most desperate of all the Indians between Oregon and Utah, was one known as Bigfoot, who, like a gigantic monster, as he truly was, roamed over the plains and mountains of Idaho with a small band of picked warriors, committing murders and depredations. They ranged from Grand Ronde Valley, in eastern Oregon, to the heads of the Owyhee and Weiser Rivers, in Idaho. Many stories were told of the great size of this noted Indian desperado, and about the size of his feet. Whenever a depredation was committed, those large moccasin tracks were certain to be found among others. He never had but few Indians with him. While the other Indians were sometimes mounted on ponies, he was always on foot. One reason for this, perhaps, was that no ordinary horse could carry him; and the following account will show that he had but little use for a horse, for the rapidity with which he traveled from place to place was the wonder and surprise to all the settlers on the Snake and Boise Rivers. One day his fresh tracks would be seen on the Weiser, and the next day he would be heard of on the Owyhee, seventy–five or eighty miles distant. Once he was chased by Wheeler, Frank Johnson, and a man by the name of Cook, who were all well mounted, while Bigfoot, as usual, was traveling on foot with two other Indians. Wheeler and his two Companions were camped near the head of the Malheur River. In the night their horses gave indications that Indians were prowling near the camp, so a close watch was kept up till daylight, when, on examination of the ground, it was discovered that old Bigfoot and two other Indians had been within a few yards of the camp during the night. Upon making this discovery all were excited—all were eager for the chase. Bigfoot had been treading on dangerous ground. Here were three as cool and determined men as ever put a foot out West, all three of them crack marksmen, and all well accustomed to Indian fighting, and three better horsemen could not have been found in the Territory. Dispatching a hasty breakfast, all mounted their horses and took the trail, Frank Johnson remarking, "Well, boys, we will make it hot for old Bigfoot to-day." Wheeler replied laughingly, "Yes; and it will make it hot for our horses to catch up with that old feather-headed devil, if he travel as far in a day as Enoch Fruit says he can." Enoch Fruit was a noted horse thief, who once kept a ferry at Farewell Bend, on Snake River, and he had often met Bigfoot and often talked and traded with him. It was through Fruit that the fact was first known that Bigfoot could speak English, and that it came to be believed that the big-footed fiend belonged to some other tribe of Indians than the one he was with, which in time proved to be true.

The three men rode on in hot pursuit. A fierce ride of two hours brought them in sight of the Indians, who were going in a rapid trot towards Snake River. All hands now prepared in earnest for the chase. The big Spanish spurs were applied without mercy, to the already bleeding flanks of their faithful and spirited horses. The two smaller Indians were soon over-taken and shot down. They made a determined and desperate resistance, but their horses and arrows and old-style guns proved of no avail before the Henry rifle in the hands of the men they had now to deal with. By the time these two Indians were dispatched, old Bigfoot was at least a mile ahead, running and jumping the sagebrush like a deer, increasing the distance between him and his pursuers where the ground was the roughest, and losing where the ground was better. The exciting chase was kept up in this way for over thirty miles with about the same result, until at last the huge monster reached Snake River and plunged into the stream, and struck out swimming for the opposite shore. He proved himself to be an excellent swimmer, as well as a skillful runner, carrying his gun and ammunition above water. The faithful horses were now put down to their best speed, but only reached the bank in time for their riders to see, much to their disappointment and disgust, the tall form of Bigfoot clambering out of the water on the other bank. Johnson shouted out, "Boys, look there; don't Bigfoot beat hell?" Cook said, "Yes; and he beat our horses, too." Wheeler quietly remarked that if old Bigfoot did not have the rheumatism after running so far and then swimming that cold river, he deserved to be remembered as a living specimen of health and endurance. In the meantime Bigfoot, having gained the bank of the river, and shaken himself, and after giving an unearthly yell, shouted out in plain English, "Come over, come over, you damned cowards," then dived into the thick willows. The poor bleeding and foaming horses were completely fagged out, and so were their riders; many times during the day the horses had plunged into badger holes, falling, and pitching their reckless riders over their heads. But those were the boys that could not be stopped by trifles; fear and failure were alike unknown to them. It was, of course, owing to rocky gullies and rough ground that Bigfoot made his wonderful escape.

Well, the next move was to go some five miles down the river, and cross at the nearest ferry, and take up the trail of the Indian again. This they did, following his enormous tracks for a few miles to the mouth of the Weiser River. Here they found that the object of their pursuit had caught two of the largest-sized salmon, and that he had built a fire and roasted them, and that he had eaten every morsel of them, leaving the bones picked clean. He had been taken the back track, and had gone to Snake River and swam back to the side from which he had been chased.

Night came on and found three of the angriest, sorest, and hungriest men who had ever lain down on Snake River. But instead of growling over their disappointment, as most men would have done, the evening was spent in joking and in recounting the many incidents of the day. It was agreed by all that old Bigfoot could out-run and out-wind any Indian on record, and that he was the largest man and that he had the largest foot by half of any man they had ever seen. That he was a dear lover of fish was evident from the skeletons he had left at his campfire. Frank Johnson said that he had a mind to have imported a first-class thoroughbred race horse that would be able to run that old yellow-legged "cuss" down or send for a pack of bloodhounds. Mr. Cook declared that if Bigfoot should happen to be as fond of dogmeat as he was of fish, that he would cut up a small pack of hounds at one meal, then swim Snake river a time or two and swallow Johnson's imported horse.

Next morning the chase was for the time abandoned. Wheeler remarking that he would get even on that old son-of-a-cricket-eater, if it took him five years, for his having caused him to ruin his fine horse, and almost breaking his own neck. This resolve was realized, but not until nearly two years afterward, during which time Bigfoot sent many a poor unfortunate miner and teamster to that land from whence no traveler returns.

Bigfoot's favorite field of slaughter was between Boise and Silver Cities, where the road passes through a narrow defile between tablerocks or

bluffs, a few miles south of Snake River. It was among these bluffs that this
noted chief and his braves lurked, and picked off many of Idaho's first
settlers. Scarcely a week passed that some one was not killed while traveling
to or from the Owyhee country. It was near this place that Bigfoot afterwards met his death in a way he least expected, just in sight of the spot
where he had murdered Mr. Ulman Lamot, a man named Baker, and a
partner of Chas. Adams. He had also shot Chas. Adams through the hand,
and had killed a score of others, whose names I do not now remember, but
the last man known to have been killed by Bigfoot and his little band was a
man named Jarvis, who was on his way from Boise Valley to Owyhee, with a
load of eggs and vegetables. A Chinaman was also killed at the same time,
who was riding with Jarvis. This occurred in 1868, just before Bigfoot himself was sent to the happy hunting-grounds by Wheeler. It thus appears that
Jarvis was Bigfoot's last victim before he met his own fate, and found more
than his match, which was no easy matter, but, like all others of his kind, he
was fated at last to meet his man.

As I am perhaps the only white man now living—unless Wheeler is still
alive—who knows how or when this noted chief Bigfoot met his death, I will
give as true and faithful an account of the thrilling and deadly encounter as
possible, and the reasons why it was kept secret from the world so long.

In the spring of 1868 I was working at the carpenters trade in Silver
City, Idaho. It was at the time of the great lawsuit, and the pitched battle,
which was fought over the Golden Chariot Quartz Lode, in which many lives
were lost on both sides, and which resulted in the death of the two owners of
the disputed ground, namely, Marion More and Samuel Lockhart. The
whole town was in an uproar and a terrible state of excitement existed.
Everybody went armed to the teeth. Governor Ballard resolved to place the
town under martial law, and many came over from Boise City to assist in the
somewhat dangerous undertaking. Among whose who came I noticed a tall,
fine-looking young man, of rather slight but handsome build, with small
hands and feet. He had dark brown hair and a smooth face, with dark, steel-
gray eyes, expressive of intelligence and a kind heart. Though there was
something striking in the appearance of the man, little did I think he could
look death in the face with a smile, or without the slightest change of
countenance, but such was the character of the man. I was made acquainted
with Wheeler by Captain Hatch, who was also a carpenter and a refined
gentlemen. He knew Wheeler well, having been on a prospecting tour with
him, and had also mined near him, or with him at one time. Wheeler was a
good-hearted fellow, and was the life of the camp, and of every circle into
which he came; but he was at the same time one of the bravest and most
determined men in the Territory. He was as strong and active as a panther,
and a better marksman than any man he ever met in his life. Though a

peaceable and temperate man, the desperadoes all knew him and never offered to infringe upon his rights. This was the last time I saw Wheeler until I met him on the scene where the terrible combat—Bigfoot's last fight—took place. This happened in the latter part of July, 1868. I was going from Silver City, to Boise City, traveling alone with a two-horse wagon. When near the dangerous pass where so many had been killed, I, being unarmed, concluded to lay over and let my horses graze until I should have company through the canyon; so I foolishly turned my horses loose and set myself to cooking something to eat. While thus engaged, the horses got frightened at something and run off, leaving me afoot and alone, and badly frightened. I followed the horses' tracks, and found they had gone down Reynolds Creek, in the direction of the massacre ground. As the creek runs through this bluff of rocks within half a mile of where the road does, I followed them, and found that they had started through the canyon, and I had just turned back, afraid to go farther, when, to my horror and surprise, I looked across the creek and saw three Indians coming at full speed. They were painted and feathered, and, as they were coming directly toward me, I felt certain that they saw me, and I thought that my time had come. The tall and terrible-looking Indian who could be none other than Bigfoot himself was some fifty yards ahead of another Indian, while the third was a equal distance behind the second one. I stood paralyzed with fear. The only chance left me was to hide behind some rocks, and there await my fate, which I felt certain would in a few minutes be death; so I crouched down behind a ledge of rocks, and bid a last farewell to home and friends, as I then thought, expecting that in a few minutes my dripping scalp would be hanging to the belt of the most horrible-looking monster I had ever beheld. It would be useless for me to attempt to describe my feelings at this moment. In less than a minute old Bigfoot came thundering along like an old buffalo bull, within less than thirty yards of me, but did not halt, making straight for the road, which was not far off. I looked and saw the stage full of passengers, with several females among the number just coming in sight.

Somewhat to my relief I now discovered that it was the stage and not myself that was the object of Bigfoot's attention. He had evidently resolved to head off the stage, and murder the driver and rob the passengers. He was destined however to do no more scalping on this side of the "dark river." When the Indian who was next to the chief was nearly opposite my hiding-place, my blood was chilled by the crack of a rifle, which dropped this Indian dead within twenty yards of me. At the report of the gun old Bigfoot jumped behind a large rock, and the hindmost Indian broke back over the hill and was not seen again. For a moment all was quiet. I saw Charley Barns, the noted stage-driver, throw the silk gracefully to his horses, as was his habit on nearing the canyon; he and his passengers all unconscious of the terrible fate they had just escaped. I afterwards learned that among the passengers were Judge Roseborough, Charley Douglass, the gambler, and Mrs. Record and her daughter. Mr. Record and family were then keeping the stage station at the Fifteen-mile House, between Boise City and Snake River. There was also among the passengers a young lady named Lib Gardner. These with Charley Barnes, the driver, made up the little company of intended victims. Little did they think that there was one so near them as I was, and in such a terrible plight, who dared not move or ask for aid, and that the most deadly and bloody encounter was about to take place that had ever been witnessed by any of us. Those few minutes seemed like hours to me, I knew that an Indian had been killed near me, but by whom, or from what direction, I could form no idea. From Bigfoot's action it was evident that he thought the report of the gun came from a tree surrounded by a clump of willows near the creek, some eighty yards from where he stood. The sequel proved that he was right. A few minutes after the stage passed out of sight, Bigfoot commenced practicing a bit of strategy that was new to me. All I could do was to lie still and in dead silence watch his movements. First he would crawl to one side of the large rock behind which he was hiding, then crawl back to the other side and cautiously peep around the side of the rock; but no one shot at him. All was dead quietude. He would then put his ear to the ground and listen, but could not hear the slightest noise. At last he tried another plan of escape. He tied a large bunch of sage-brush to his back and tried to crawl away; and to my great horror he was advancing directly toward the spot where I lay hidden behind a ledge of rocks. He came slowly and gently toward me. I was undecided whether to remain where I was a while longer, or jump and run toward the clump of willows which Bigfoot had been watching so long, and take the chances of finding a white man. If I remained where I was much longer, Bigfoot, who had not yet seen me, could not fail to find me; but this terrible state of suspense was soon brought to an end. When Bigfoot had crawled over about half the distance that separated his hiding-place from mine, I heard a clear voice ring out on the mountain air, in cool, deliberate tones, saying: "Get up from there, Bigfoot, you old feather-headed, leather-bellied coward. I can see you crawling off like a snake. Here is a scalp; come down and take mine, you coward." At this Bigfoot sprang to his feet, and leveled a large, double-barreled rifle at the willows, and said : "You coward; me no coward. You come out; I'll scalp you, too." At this Wheeler sprang out from among the bushes in plain view, saying: "Here I am, now sail in old rooster." Both men fired almost at the same instant. Bigfoot staggered, but recovered and fired again, and then threw his gun down and started to run toward the dead Indian. He ran but a few yards, when another shot caused him to reel again, but he succeeded in reaching the spot where the dead Indian lay, and, picking up the gun left by the latter where he had fallen, he leveled it toward Wheeler and fired again, just at the moment that Wheeler's gun sent another unerring bullet into his powerful frame. Bigfoot again staggered and came very near falling, but again recovered, and, drawing a knife, gave an unearthly whoop, which almost froze my blood, and then started toward Wheeler. He had gone but a few yards when another shot staggered him, and then another. I was dumb with fear, apprehending that after all the Indian might succeed in reaching Wheeler and then grasp him in his powerful clutches. Wheeler never moved from the spot where he stood, but, handling his gun with extraordinary skill, continued to fire, until at last, when within thirty yards of him, the huge red demon fell with a broken leg to rise no more. Wheeler, however, emptied the balance of the sixteen shots into him, and then, without moving out of his tracks, reloaded his rifle and said: "How do you like the way my gun shoots, old hoss? I'll bet my scalp against yours that you don't scalp any more white men in this canyon very soon." Bigfoot cried out in plain English, "Don't shoot me any more, you have killed me." Wheeler walked up near the Indian, and, pulling out an ivory-handled revolver, gazed a moment at his fallen foes, then shouted out to me, "Come down, whoever you are; there is no danger now." I went to the spot and found Bigfoot bleeding from twelve wounds, both legs and one arm broken. The Indian asked for water when Wheeler said: "Hold on till I break that other arm; then I'll give you a drink." Bigfoot said: "Well, do it quick, and give me a drink and let me die." Wheeler leveled his pistol, and at the report the arm fell useless to the ground. This to some may seem cruel, but I was yet afraid to go near this powerful and desperate savage monster. Wheeler went down to the creek, and brought up his canteen full of water, and placed it to the mouth of the Indian, who drank it all. Bigfoot then said he wished he had some whisky, when Wheeler said he had a small bottle of whisky and ammonia, which be always carried in case of snake bites; that he could have that if he thought it would do him any good. Bigfoot said; "Give it to me, quick; I'm getting blind." Wheeler gave him a pint flask, filled with the strong fluid, mixed with a little water. The Indian drank it, every drop, and then said : "I'm sick and blind," and then fell back apparently dead. After a few minutes he revived, and said that he was better, and that he wished us to wash the dust and paint from his face, and see what a good-looking man he was. We complied with his request, and to our surprise, we found a fine-looking face, with the handsomest set of teeth we ever beheld. He had large, black, but wicked-looking eyes. His complexion had been almost white, but was now of course badly tanned. He had a heavy shock of long black hair, somewhat inclined to be kinky. He was of enormous size, and such hands, and especially feet, I never saw on any mortal before or since. He soon began to be quite talkative, and expressed a wish that we would make him one promise.

Wheeler asked him what it was. He asked that we should not scalp him, nor take him to Boise after he died, but to drag him in among the willows, and pile some rocks upon him, and to lay his gun by his side. "If you will promise me this," he said, "I shall die satisfied." Wheeler told him that if he would tell him who he was, and where he came from, he would perhaps promise, and do what he wished; but that he must answer all the questions he was asked, and tell the truth. Bigfoot then said: "I have been a very bad man; and if I tell you all that I have done, I am afraid you will not do what I have asked of you." Wheeler said: "I know you have been a bad man, but if you will tell me everything, I will not tell any one that you are dead, nor tell anything about you." When Wheeler said this, Bigfoot seemed to brighten up and said: "Now do keep your promise, and I will tell you my whole history, and all that I have gone through, if I can only live long enough to do so." Wheeler said: "I have been assured by prominent citizens of Boise that if any one killed you and brought your feet and your scalp to Fort Boise, at least $1,000 would be paid for them, for you have done a great deal of mischief; killed many white people, and everybody thinks that you were one of the party that killed Mrs. Scott and her husband on Burnt River last fall, as your big tracks were found next day near the scene of the murder, as they have always been found when white people have been killed by Indians in this part of the country. I have now been out here four days waiting for you, and the mosquitoes have nearly eaten me up while hiding in the willows, but now, if it will do you any good, I will hide you, but I will break your gun so that other Indians will not use it again."

BIGFOOT'S HISTORY AND CONFESSION

The following is Bigfoot's account of himself and his career, taken down just as it was related to Wheeler and myself:

"I was born in the Cherokee nation. My father was a white man named Archer Wilkinson. He was hanged for murder in the Cherokee nation when I was a small boy. My mother was part Cherokee and part negro, so I was told. She was a good Christian woman. My name is Starr Wilkinson. I was thus named after Thomas Starr, a noted desperado in the nation. I was always called Bigfooted Wilkinson as long ago as I can remember. The boys always made fun of me when I was a boy, because I was so large for my age, and had such big feet. I had a bad temper, and got to drinking when quite young, and got to be so strong that when any one would call me a nickname I would fight him. In this way, I came near killing several with my fist. I found out that I would soon be killed if I remained in that county, so I ran away from home, and went to Tiloqua, then the capital of the Cherokee nation. There I fell in with some emigrants, who were going to Oregon in 1856, and drove a team across the plains, for my board. The folks I traveled with were very kind to me. I fell in love with a young lady of the company, who thought a good deal of me until we fell in with company from New York. Along with these new people was an artist, who was a smart, good-looking fellow. He soon cut me out. After this the young lady would hardly notice me or speak to me. I knew then that he had told her something bad about me. He made fun of me several times, and, while we were camped near the Goose Creek Mountains, he and I went out one morning to hunt up the stock. We went to the bank of Snake River. I asked him what he intended to do when he got to Oregon. He said he was going to marry my girl and settle down. I told him he should not do so; for I thought I had the best right to her. He only laughed and said: "Do you suppose she would marry a bigfooted nigger like you, and throw off a good-looking fellow like me?" This made me mad, and I told him I was no negro, and that if he called me that again I would kill him. So he drew his gun on me, and repeated it again. I was unarmed, but started at him. He shot me in the side but did not hurt me much; so I grabbed him and threw him down, and choked him to death, then threw him into Snake River, took his gun, pistol, and knife, and ran off into the hills.

The emigrants did not leave camp for a few days. They were, perhaps, hunting for us. Some of them went on to Oregon, but the family that I had been traveling with went back with some others to Salt Lake, where they wintered. I made my way to the Boise River, where I found a French trader and trapper, and a man named Joe Lewis, who had been with the Indians for many years. This Joe Lewis was one who helped massacre Doctor Whitman and many others near old Walla Walla, in 1847. He was a bad man, but he was a good friend to me when I needed a friend. So I went with him and joined the Indians, and have been with them ever since. In 1857 I went with Lewis and some Indians near the emigrant road for the purpose of stealing stock from the emigrants. In one of our raids, I found cattle that I knew had belonged to the family I had crossed the plains with the year before. So I determined to go to the train and see if my girl was with them, and try to get her to run off with me. I found her, but she was very mad with me, as were all the rest. They said they thought I had killed Mr. Hart, the young artist, and that I ought to hang for it. They told me to leave the camp. I told the girl that if she did not have me she would be sorry for it before she reached Oregon. I had to leave, but was determined to have revenge; so I took Joe Lewis and thirty Indians, and followed down Boise River, where it empties into Snake River, and massacred them, and run off all their stock. I and several Indians ravished the girl before we killed her. I am sorry for that

now, for she was a good girl; but it is too late now to be sorry. I was mad
and foolish. I have been in several other massacres. I helped to kill the
Scott family on Burnt River. We wanted their horses. I also helped to kill
an officer, and took his wife prisoner last fall. The officer was on his way to
Camp Lyon. His wife got sick, had a child and could not ride; so some of
the Indians killed her. I had a squaw for a wife, and when Jeff Stanford was
out with a lot of men fighting us, they killed my wife, and carried off my little
boy. Since that time I have done all the mischief I could, and am glad of it."
Wheeler here asked Bigfoot what became of Joe Lewis. He said that Lewis
was shot by a man who carried the express from Auburn to Boise in 1862.
While Lewis was trying to steal some horses on the Payette River one night
the expressman shot across the river with buckshot, hitting Lewis in the side
and wounding Bigfoot in the leg. As it was dark, and neither of the
wounded men spoke, the expressman did not know that any one had been
hit. "Joe whispered to me," continued Bigfoot, "that he was hurt bad; so I
took him on my back and started to run with him, but he soon died, and I
covered him up in the sand on the banks of the Payette River where he was
never found by the whites; and that was the last of poor Joe, and I hope you
will do that much for me." Wheeler said:, "All right, Mr. Wilkinson. I guess
I will do it, as I am from the Cherokee nation myself, and have a little
Cherokee blood in my veins. I will not refuse to grant your dying request."
When Wheeler said this and assured him that he would not take his body or
any portion of it to the fort, Bigfoot actually wept, and asked to know
Wheeler's name, and said: "You are a brave man, and I know you will keep
your word. I am a brave man too, but you shot a little too quick for me, and
you had the best gun and you have killed me. Your shot struck me just as I
was pulling the trigger else I think I should have killed you, as I hardly ever
missed anything I ever shot at. I got my old gun at the massacre in 1857. I
do not know how many men I have killed with it. I knew I was killed when
your first shot struck me; for I could not see to shoot well afterwards."

Bigfoot was throwing up blood every few minutes and bleeding fast
from his numerous wounds, half of which would have proved sufficient to
kill any ordinary man instantly, but he was possessed of so much vigor and
vitality that he lived for nearly two hours after receiving so many mortal
wounds. Wheeler asked where the Indians got their ammunition. He said
that some of it was obtained from friendly Indians, who visited the towns and
military posts for that purpose. Bigfoot continued: "Nearly all of my little
bad of warriors are killed off. There are but five left who have been running
with me. You have just killed one of the bravest of the band. He has been
one of my head braves ever since the Indians recognized me as the leader of
the brave little band. His father is the old medicine man, and he told me
when we left not to go on this trip; for he had dreamed about us. He

dreamed that there was a large snake secreted in these bluffs that had a white man's head on, and had a medicine gun; that when he pointed it at the Indians they could not see how to shoot and that after killing them he broke their guns to pieces. He wept when we left camp and said that he would never see us again until we met in the spirit land. He was right. If I had minded him I would not have got killed." Wheeler said: "Well, if you meet the old medicine gentleman in the spirit land tell him he was a good hand at dreaming, if he did call me a snake." Wheeler then asked him where the rest of the Indians were camped. Bigfoot said: "This is something I cannot tell; but I will tell you anything you may ask me. There are but few of them left; and now that we are killed, the rest will soon go into the fort and it would do you no good to kill them. The little band I run with call themselves Piutes; the rest call themselves 'Fish Indians,' because they live by fishing on the Malheur and Snake rivers and do not mix with the Lake Piutes and Bannocks. The other Indians are not friendly toward us, and I care nothing about them; but our little band have been brave Indians. They have always treated me well, and I do not wish to betray them as the last act of a bad life." Wheeler said: "Bully for you, Wilkinson. I think more of you than I did before, for you are not a traitor if you have been a bad Indian otherwise." Wheeler asked him how tall he was and how much he thought he weighed. Bigfoot said he did not know; for he had grown very much since he joined the Indians; that when he left the whites he was but nineteen years old; that he then measured six feet six and a half inches in height and weighted 255 pounds. "But I know," he said, "that I must weigh at least 300 pounds now, and there is not a pound of fat on me," which was true. He was a model of strength and endurance. I had a tape line and rule in my pocket with which I took the following exact measurements of this wonderful being: Around the chest, 59 inches; height, 6 feet 8 1/2 inches; length of foot, 17 1/2 inches; around the ball of the foot, 18 inches; around the widest part of the hand, 18 inches. I am confident that he must have weighed at least 300 pounds, and all bone and sinew; not a pound of surplus flesh on him. We asked him if he knew how strong he was. He said: "No; but I was very powerful. I have had as many as ten Indians at me trying to throw me down, but they never succeeded. I have many times run all day long without being hurt by it; but I have suffered a great deal from hunger, for this is a poor game country." Wheeler asked him if he knew any other white man besides Enoch Fruit, who had been mixed up with the Indians. Bigfoot said that there was a man called Washoe Charley, who had lived with the Indians for awhile, and then stole all their best horses and ran off to the whites again. He then began to tell us about the assisting in the killing of man named Jordan, who he said had helped to kill Indian squaws and children because some other Indians had stolen his horses. He said that Jordan was a very bad man, but that he was a good fighter. His voice here failed him, and he fell back saying, "Everything is getting dark," and lay silent for awhile, then spoke in husky, rapid tones, "Look! Look! The soldiers are after me! I must go quick, quick!" He then straightened out and died without a struggle.

We both stood and gazed at the dead body for a moment in silence. Two hours before, the gigantic chief had struck terror to the heart, and now he lay lifeless and harmless at my feet, all covered with blood and the ground all around him saturated by the crimson tide. This being the first time I had ever witnessed such a thing, the reader must be left to imagine my feelings. Wheeler talked the whole affair over as unconcernedly as though nothing unusual had happened, remarking that according to Bigfoot's story, that he was but 31 years old, though he looked to be much older, and that he was quite large enough to be on hundred years old. I asked Wheeler what we should do next. He said: "We will first break their guns to pieces, unless you want one of them." I told him they would be useless to me, as I could not shoot. So Wheeler said, "In order that the old medicine man may not be made out a liar, I will break them over this rock." This he did, and bent the barrels so that they could not be used again. We then went and looked up my horses, put a rope around Bigfoot's body, to which we hitched the horses, and dragged the body some one hundred and fifty yards to the creek, and put Bigfoot's old broken gun by his side. We then threw some brush and rocks upon him, hid the other broken gun, threw away what little ammunition the dead Indians had left, and left the other Indian lying where he had fallen. Wheeler said the other Indians would probably come and burn what they could find, if they were not afraid to try it.

We left the spot and went to my wagon, where we had something to eat, as Wheeler was very hungry, having eaten nothing for two days. We then started for Boise City, where we arrived the next day. Wheeler made me promise to say nothing about the affair, as he had given his word to Bigfoot, and was resolved not to break the promise he had made. I left Idaho a few days afterward for Nevada; but I still have in my tool-chest one of Bigfoot's moccasins, which is a curiosity well worth looking at.

I have never heard of Wheeler since, and never—until now—mentioned the affair to any one. The day I left Boise City I saw Wheeler very neatly dressed, sitting and conversing quietly with some gentlemen. He did not appear at all like the man who, three days before, had met and killed in fair combat two of the most desperate of all the braves of Idaho, and a deed which would have been proudly boasted of by almost any other man, was kept a secret from the world by the singular but brave Wheeler.

As I have now given as truthful an account of this whole affair as possible, I hope that after so many years have passed that I have done no one any harm in telling what I knew of the terrible encounter between these two

Bigfoot Statue

By Old Fort Boise Replica, Parma, ID.

Photo by Author, 16 July 2007.

Epilogue

ON THE OREGON TRAIL

Out on the desert, barren and wide,
  Watered along by the immigrant tears;
Upon the Oregon Trail she died—
  Rebecca Winter, aged fifty years.
Seeking the land of the storied West
  Opulent land of gold and fame,
Leaving her hearthstone warm, with the rest,
  From somewhere out of the East, she came.

Maybe the heart in her bosom died
  For grief for some little grave back home,
Leaving all for the man at her side,
  For women must follow, where man would roam.

'Twas famine, or fever, or wan despair
  That hushed the cry of her silent breast;
Close by the trail, where the wagons fare,
  Rebecca Winter was laid to rest.
Somebody—husband, son, or sire—
  Roughly wrought, seeing not for tears,
This, for her grave, on a sunken tire:
  "Rebecca Winter—aged 50 years."

Long she lay by the Oregon Trail,
  With sagebrush growing above her head,
And coyotes barked in the moonlight pale,
  And wagon-trains moved on by the dead.

Till, bearing compass and line and chain,
  Men came, marking a way to the West,
Daring the desert's drought and the pain,
  A daring heart in each dauntless breast.
And stumbling into a sagebrush bed,
  The lineman read—through a mist of tears—
On the wagon tire, that marked her head,
  "Rebecca Winter—aged 50 years."

"Boys," said the leader, "we'll turn aside,
  Here, close by the trail, her grave shall stay,
For she came first in this desert wide,
  Rebecca Winter holds right of way."

Today[1] the train glides fast to the West,
  Rounding the curve where the grave appears;
A white shaft marking her place of rest,
  "Rebecca Winter—aged 50 years."
Here is the shapen[2] and turf-grown mound,
  And the name carved on the stone today;
But the thought—"'Tis for all the graves unfound,
  The others, who died upon the way."
                   —Anne McQueen[3]

    "Rebecca Winters was a 50-year-old Latterday Saint who died of cholera in 1852. Her grave was marked by an iron wheel rim inscribed with her name." In early September 1995, "the Burlington Northern railroad dug up and moved the grave of pioneer Rebecca Winters near Scottsbluff, Nebraska. The tracks originally detoured around the grave site, but the railroad wants to run another line and the current location of the grave raised safety concerns, since visitors had to cross the tracks from the highway to visit the site."[4]

Notes

Abbreviations used in Text

Those major sources of information for *Massacre Rocks and City of Rocks*, that are sequentially dated in diaries, journals, manuscripts, and published accounts, are mainly cited in the text by a letter in superscript, instead of being referenced with an Arabic numeral:

B   Sherlock Bristol, "Chapter XVI: Across the Plains to Oregon," The *Pioneer Preacher* (Chicago: Fleming H. Revell, 1887).

J   Henry M. Judson, Diary of 1862: Omaha to Oregon, Nebraska State Historical Society, #358, Ms. 953.

G   Jane A. Gould, *Jane A. Gould, Her Journal* (American Falls ID: Dan's Printing for Friends of Massacre Rock, 1984).

H   John C. Hileman, Letter to Mrs. Bronson [Marion W. Brownson], Snake River, August 11, 1862, as interposed in the copy of Hamilton Scott's diary, "Trip Across Plains in 1862," Moscow: University of Idaho, Special Collections.

JM   James S. McClung, diary, 1862, Idaho Historical Society, MS 0766, Box 3, Folder 18.

EM   Evans S. McComas, *A Journal of Travel* [1862] (Portland, OR: Champoeg Press, 1954).

HS   Hamilton Scott, "Trip Across Plains in 1862," Copy of diary, Moscow ID: University of Idaho, Special Collections.

RS   Robert C. Scott, "Robert C. Scott's Trip To Washington With Oxen in 1862," diary, January 12, 1863, furnished by E. L. Scott, Boise: Idaho State Historical Society, MS 2/466.

Chapter 1

1. Foregoing and following from Medorem Crawford, *Journal of Medorem Crawford* [1842] (Fairfield, WA: Ye Galleon Press, 1967).
2. Crawford, 1842 Journal.
3. Crawford, 1842 Journal; John D. Unruh, Jr., *The Plains Across* (Urbana: Univ. of Illinois Press, 1979), 84.
4. A.B. Roberts, "Fragments of Early History," *Up To The Times* (Walla Walla Publishing), March–April 1911, 3288–3292, 3345–3349.
5. Foregoing from A.B. Roberts.
6. Foregoing from A.B. Roberts.
7. Foregoing from A.B. Roberts

Chapter 2

1. Unruh, 85.
2. George Chandler, "Some Pioneer Experiences of George Chandler," W. B. Chandler, editor, *Oregon Historical Quarterly*, 66: March-December 1965, pp. 197–99.
3. "June 16–October 30, 1862.—Emigrant Road expedition from Omaha, Ter., to Portland, Oreg.," *War of the Rebellion*, Series I, Vol. L, Part I, 153–155 hereafter cited as Crawford 1862 Report; Captain Medorem Crawford, Report and Journal of 1862, 37th Congress, 3rd Session, Senate, *Ex. Doc. No. 17* (Ser. 1149), 1–14 hereafter cited as Crawford 1862 Journal.

4. Medorem Crawford, Samuel Gillespie Crawford (father), Leroy Crawford (brother), and R. B. Ironsides, Journalist, "Crawford Journals—1861-1864," Yale University: Beinecke Library, WA Mss 116, hereafter cited as Crawford, 1861-64; Crawford 1862 Journal.

5. Foregoing from Crawford, 1862 Report.

6. *Massacre Rocks Historical Leaflet* (Massacre Rocks State Park, American Falls ID: Friends of Massacre Rocks, c1985).

7. H.F. Swasley, *Quincy* (IL) *Union*, 28 October 1862 as quoted in "Massacre Rocks," *Reference Series 234* (Boise: Idaho Historical Society, Revised 1985).

8. Louisa J. Paul Estes, "Reminiscences of Mrs. Louisa J. Estes at age of 75 of her trip across the Plains over the Old Oregon Trail by Ox team, 1862," Idaho Historical Society, MS 0766, Box 3, Folder 19.

9. Louisa Paul Estes.

10. Philip O. Olsen, "Covered Wagons Real to Her," Interview of Mrs. Christena Chambers, *Portland Sunday Oregonian Magazine,* 19 February 1950. Clipping, Pioneer Biography File 2, Malheur County Library, hereafter cited as Chambers.

11. Margaret A. Stoot Ewing Thiel, "Mrs. Margaret A. Thiel Relates Thrilling Story of Perils of the Plains in 1862," Idaho Historical Society, MS 0766, Box 3, Folder 18.

12. Thiel.

13. Merrill J. Mattes, *Platte River Road Narratives* (Urbana, IL: University of Illinois Press, 1988), 549.

14. Daniel McLaughlin, *Sketch of A Trip From Omaha to Salmon River* (Fairfield, WA: Ye Galleon Press, 1976).

Chapter 3

1. Alvin Zaring, Notes added to Hamilton Scott's diary, *American Falls* (ID) *Power County Press*, 7, 14, 21 & 28 July 1949.

2. Oliver B. Slater, "Reminiscences of O. B. Slater," Idaho Historical Society, MS 0766, Box 4, Folder 5.

3. Slater.

4. Slater.

5. Mattes, *Narratives*, 553.

6. Slater.

7. Slater.

8. Mattes, *Narratives*, 553.

9. Zaring.

10. Crawford, 1862 Journal.

11. Zaring.

12. Crawford, 1862 Report.

13. Henry R. Herr, "Extracts fom Diary," Portland: Oregon Historical Society, Mss 1508—Miscl. Overland Journeys to the Pacific.

Chapter 4

1. McLaughlin.

2. McLaughlin.

3. William Purvine, "Letters from Powder River," *Salem Oregon States-man*, 13 October 1862.

4. "Almo Massacre," *Reference Series 232* (Boise: Idaho Historical Society, Revised February 1971).

5. "Almo Massacre."

6. Purvine.

7. "Almo Massacre."

8. Crawford, 1862 Journal.

9. Herr.

10. Crawford, 1862 Report.

11. Herr.

12. Herr.

13. Chandler.

14. Chandler.

15. Foregoing from McLaughlin.

16. McLaughlin.

17. "Attacks by Indians on Immigrants on the Plains," *San Francisco Evening Bulletin*, 27 September 1862, hereafter cited as *SFB*.

Chapter 5

1. *Massacre Rocks State Park* (Massacre Rocks State Park, American Falls ID: Friends of Massacre Rocks, c1985).

2. *Massacre Rocks State Park*; Aubrey L. Haines, *Historic Sites Along the Oregon Trail* (Gerald MO: Patrice Press, 1981).

3. "Massacre Rocks," *Reference Series 927* (Boise: Idaho Historical Society, April 1995).

4. *Massacre Rocks State Park*; "Massacre Rocks," *RS 927*; *Massacre Rocks Historical Leaflet*.

5. *Massacre Rocks Historical Leaflet*.

6. Chambers.

7. Zaring.

8. Charles M. Harrison, letter to *Iowa City State Press*, in "Early Day Indian Fight," *Idaho City World*, 31 March 1911.

9. *Massacre Rocks Historical Leaflet*.

10. Foregoing and following from Harrison.

11. William Redhoffer, account in "Indian Depredations on the Plains," *Walla Walla Washington Statesman*, 4 October 1862.

12. Swasley.

13. *Massacre Rocks Historical Leaflet*.

14. Harrison.

15. Foregoing and following from Swasley; and and *SFB*.

16. Thiel.

17. Foregoing and following from Swasley; and and *SFB*.

18. Redhoffer.

19. Thiel.

20. Redhoffer.
21. *SFB.*

Chapter 6

1. Redhoffer.
2. Harrison.
3. Swasley; Redhoffer.
4. *SFB.*
5. *SFB.*
6. Harrison.

Chapter 7

1. Redhoffer.
2. Harrison; Swasley.
3. *Massacre Rocks Historical Leaflet.*
4. Louisa Paul Estes.
5. Harrison; Redhoffer.
6. Swasley.

Chapter 8

1. Swasley
2. Foregoing from Harrison.
3. Foregoing from H.F. Swasley
4. "City of Rocks and Granite Pass," *Reference Series 126* (Boise: Idaho Historical Society, revised 1993).
5. Following from "Maps and Reports of Fort Kearney, South Pass, and Honey Lake Wagon Road," 37th Congress, 2nd Session, Vol. 9, 1861–62, House, *Ex. Doc. No 64* (Ser. 1100), 1–26, hereafter cited as Lander's report.

6. Foregoing and following from Lander's report.

7. Foregoing from Lander's report.

8. "City of Rocks and Granite Pass," *RS 126*; "Almo's Indian Legend" *Reference Series 1049* (Boise: Idaho Historical Society, August 1995).

Chapter 9

1. "City of Rocks and Granite Pass," *RS 126*.

2. Swasley.

3. "Massacre Rocks," *Reference Series 234* (Boise: Idaho Historical Society, Revised 1985).

4. *Virginia City* (NV) *Territorial Enterprise,* 1 October 1862, in "Almo Massacre," Reference Series 232 (Boise: Idaho Historical Society, Revised February 1971).

5. "Massacre Rocks," *RS 234*.

6. "More Arrivals," *Sacramento Daily Union*, 4 October 1862.

7. "Massacre Rocks," *RS 234*.

8. Following from "More Arrivals," *SDU*.

9. Foregoing from Swasley.

10. *SFB*.

Chapter 10

1. "Another Attack On Emigrants by Indians—Six Men Killed," *Salt Lake City Deseret News*, 24 September 1862.

2. *Deseret News*, 24 September 1862.

3. Foregoing from *Deseret News*, 24 September 1862.

4. Foregoing from *Deseret News*, 24 September 1862.

5. Foregoing from *Deseret News*, 24 September 1862.

6. Foregoing from *Deseret News*, 24 September 1862.

7. Foregoing from *Deseret News*, 24 September 1862.

8. Foregoing from "Great Suffering and Tenacity of Life," *Salt Lake City Deseret News*, 26 November 1862.

9. Foregoing from *Deseret News*, 26 November 1862.

10. Foregoing from *Deseret News*, 26 November 1862.

11. Foregoing from *Deseret News*, 26 November 1862.

12. Foregoing from "Massacre Rocks," *RS 234*.

13. "City of Rocks and Granite Pass," *RS 126*; "Pocatello hopes Shoshone leader's statue draws tourists," *Idaho Press-Tribune* (Nampa, ID), 18 June 2007.

Chapter 11

1. Crawford, 1862 Report.

2. Crawford, 1862 Journal.

3. McLaughlin.

4. Crawford, 1862 Journal.

Chapter 12

The sources of information for this chapter are from Sherlock Bristol; Henry Judson; Evans McComas; Hamilton Scott; and Robert Scott.

Chapter 13

1. Zaring; Orders, No. 140, Fort Walla Walla, 21 July 1862, and Orders, No. 142, Fort Walla Walla, 22 July 1862, *War of the Rebellion*, Series I, Vol. L, Part II, 35.

2. B/Gen Benjamin Alvord to Governor of Washington Ter., Fort Vancouver, 28 July 1862, *War of the Rebellion*, Series I, Vol. L, Part II, 42–43.

3. Zaring.

4. Slater.

5. Slater, and following

6. Foregoing from Dunham Wright, "Old Timer Tells of Privations in Real Early Days," Boise *Idaho Statesman*, 2 March 1919.

7. Thiel.

Chapter 14

1. Purvine.

2. Alvin Zaring; Thiel;

3. Crawford, 1862 Report, and following.

4. Crawford, 1862 Journal.

5. Crawford, 1862 Report.

6. McLaughlin.

7. Mattes, *Narratives*, 543.

8. Wright.

Appendix I

1. "Almo's Indian Legend," *RS 1049,* and following.

2. "Almo's Indian Legend," *RS 1049,* and following.

3. "Almo's Indian Legend," *RS 1049,* and following.

4. Charles Shirley Walgamott, "Writer Says Almo Massacre Was Most Important Indian Disaster In Idaho," *100 Years of Progress Edition*, Burley *South Idaho Press*, August 1970.

5. Walgamott.

6. Frederick M. Huchel, *A history of Box Elder County*, (Salt Lake City: Utah State Historical Society, 1999), pp 158–59.

7. Huchel.

Appendix II

1. Foregoing and following from "Bigfoot," *Reference Series 40* (Boise: Idaho Historical Society, March 1982).

2. Annie Laurie Bird, "Origin of the Name Nampa," *Reference Series 39* (Boise: Idaho Historical Society, May 1966).

3. Foregoing from "Bigfoot," *RS 40*.

4. Foregoing from "Bigfoot," *RS 40*.

5. "Bigfoot," *RS 40*.

6. "The Noted Indian Bigfoot," *History of Idaho Territory* (San Francisco: Wallace W. Elliott and Company, 1884), pp 144–.

7. *Idaho Statesman*, 24 June 1880.

8. *Idaho Statesman*, 22 June 1880.

9. *Idaho Statesman*, 18 May and 22 May 1880.

10. "Bigfoot," *RS 40*.

11. "The Giant and the Gunslinger," *True*, September 1957, p 57–.

12. "The Bigfooted Fiend," *Idaho Statesman*, 14 November 1878.

Epilogue

1. Prior to 1920.

2. *Webster*: "fashioned in or provided with a definite shape."

3. James H. Hawley, *History of Idaho: The Gem of the Mountains,* Chicago S.J. Clarke, 1920, 81–82.

4. Will Bagley, "Railroad Relocates Rebecca Winters Grave," *News from the Plains, October 1995,* Newsletter of the Oregon-California Trails Association, Independence, MO.

Bibliography

"Almo's Indian Legend." *Reference Series 1049.* Boise: Idaho Historical Society, August 1995.

"Almo Massacre." *Reference Series 232.* Boise: Idaho Historical Society, Revised February 1971.

"Alvin Zaring." *Portland Oregonian*, 22 November 1929.

"Attacks by Indians on Immigrants on the Plains." *Evening Bulletin* (San Francisco), 27 September 1862.

"Bigfoot." *Reference Series 40.* Boise: Idaho Historical Society, 1982.

Bird, Annie Laurie. "Origin of the Name Nampa." *Reference Series 39.* Boise: Idaho Historical Society, May 1966.

Boise *Idaho Statesman*, 1878, 1880, 1919.

Bristol, Sherlock. *The Pioneer Preacher.* Chicago: Fleming H. Revell, 1887.

Brown, Jennie Broughton. *Fort Hall on the Oregon Trail.* Caldwell, ID: Caxton, 1932.

Burley (ID) *South Idaho Press*, 1970.

"Covered Wagons Real to Her." Interview of Mrs. Christena Chambers by Philip O. Olsen, 19 February 1940 clipping. Pioneer Biography File 2. Malheur County Library, Ontario, Oregon.

Chandler, George. "Some Pioneer Experiences of George Chandler." W.B. Chandler, editor. *Oregon Historical Quarterly*, 66: March-December 1965.

"City of Rocks and Granite Pass." *Reference Series 126.* Boise: Idaho Historical Society, revised 1993.

Crawford, Medorem. *Journal of Medorem Crawford* [1842]. Fairfield, WA: Ye Galleon Press, 1967.

Crawford, Medorem; Samuel Gillespie Crawford; Leroy Crawford; and R. B. Ironsides, Journalist. "Crawford Journals—1861-1864," Yale University: Beinecke Library, WA Mss 116.

Estes, Louisa J. Paul. "Reminiscences of Mrs. Louisa J. Estes at age of 75 of her trip across the Plains over the Old Oregon Trail by Ox team, 1862." Idaho Historical Society, MS 0766, Box 3, Folder 19.

Gould, Jane A. *Jane A. Gould, Her Journal.* American Falls, ID: Dan's Printing for Friends of Massacre Rock, 1984.

Haines, Aubrey L. *Historic Sites Along the Oregon Trail.* Gerald, MO: Patrice Press, 1981.

Harrison, Charles M. Letter to *Iowa City State Press.* Quoted in "Early Day Indian Fight." *Idaho World,* (Idaho City) 31 March 1911.

Hawley, James H. *History of Idaho: The Gem of the Mountains.* Chicago: S.J. Clarke, 1920.

Hileman, John C. Letter to Mrs. Bronson [Marion W. Brownson], Snake River, August 11, 1862. As interposed in the copy of Hamilton Scott's diary, "Trip Across Plains in 1862." Moscow: University of Idaho, Special Collections.

History of Box Elder County. Salt Lake City: Utah State Historical Society, 1999.

History of Idaho Territory. San Francisco: Wallace W. Elliott and Company, 1884.

Huchel, Frederick M. *A History of Box Elder County.* Salt Lake City: Utah State Historical Society, 1999.

Judson, Henry M. Diary of 1862: Omaha to Oregon. RG0953.AM: Henry M. Judson collection, Nebraska State Historical Society.

Madsen, Brigham D. *Chief Pocatello: The 'White Plume'.* Salt Lake City: University of Utah Press, 1986.

"The Massacre Near American Falls." Salt Lake City *Deseret News,* 26 November 1862.

Massacre Rocks State Park. Massacre Rocks State Park, American Falls ID: Friends of Massacre Rocks, c1985.

"Massacre Rocks." *Reference Series 234.* Boise: Idaho Historical Society, Revised 1985.

"Massacre Rocks." *Reference Series 927.* Boise: Idaho Historical Society, April 1995.

Massacre Rocks Historical Leaflet. Massacre Rocks State Park, American Falls ID: Friends of Massacre Rocks, c1985.

Mattes, Merrill J. *Platte River Road Narratives.* Urbana, IL: University of Illinois Press, 1988.

McComas, Evans S. *A Journal of Travel [1862].* Portland, OR: Champoeg Press, 1954.

McClung, James S. Diary 1862. Idaho Historical Society, MS 0766, Box 3, Folder 18.

McLaughlin, Daniel. *Sketch of A Trip From Omaha to Salmon River.* Fairfield, WA: Ye Galleon Press, 1976.

News from the Plains. Newsletter of the Oregon-California Trails Associa-tion, Independence, MO, October 1995.

Olsen, Philip O. "Covered Wagons Real to Her." Interview of Mrs. Christena Chambers. 19 February 1940 clipping, Pioneer Biography File 2, Malheur County Library.

Purvine, William. "Letters from Powder River." *Salem Oregon Statesman*, 13 October 1862.

Roberts, A.B. "Fragments of Early History." *Up To The Times* (Walla Walla Publishing), March–April 1911.

Redhoffer, William. "Indian Depredations on the Plains." *Washington Statesman* (Walla Walla, WA), 4 October 1862.

Sacramento Daily Union, 1862.

Salt Lake City Deseret News. 1862.

San Francisco Evening Bulletin, 27 September 1862.

Scott, Hamilton. "Trip Across Plains in 1862." Copy of diary. Moscow: University of Idaho, Special Collections.

———. Diary and notes by Alvin Zaring. "A Trip Across the

Plains in 1862." *Power County Press* (American Falls ID), 7, 14, 21 & 28 July 1949.

Scott, Robert C. "Robert C. Scott's Trip To Washington With Oxen in 1862." Diary, January 12, 1863, furnished by E.L. Scott, Boise: Idaho State Historical Society, MS 2/466.

Swasley, H.F. *Union* (Quincy, IL), 28 October 1862. As quoted in "Massacre Rocks," *Reference Series 234* (Boise: Idaho Historical Society, Revised 1985).

Thiel, Margaret A. Stoot Ewing. "Mrs. Margaret A. Thiel Relates Thrilling Story of Perils of the Plains in 1862." Idaho Historical Society, MS 0766, Box 3, Folder 18.

True magazine, September 1957.

Unruh, John D., Jr. *The Plains Across*. Urbana: University of Illinois Press, 1979.

Virginia City, Nevada *Territorial Enterprise*, 1862.

Walgamott, Charles Shirley. "Writer Says Almo Massacre Was Most Important Indian Disaster In Idaho." *100 Years of Progress Edition*. Burley (ID) *South Idaho Press*, August 1970.

Zaring, Alvin. Notes added to Hamilton Scott's diary. *Power County Press* (American Falls ID), 7, 14, 21 & 28 July 1949.

US Congress. House. 37th Cong., 2nd sess., 1861–62. "Maps and Reports of Fort Kearney, South Pass, and Honey Lake Wagon Road." Vol. 9, *Ex. Doc. No 64*. Serial 1100.

US Congress. Senate. 37th Congress, 3rd Session.

———. Captain Medorem Crawford. Report and Journal of 1862. *Ex. Doc. No. 17*, 1–14. Serial 1149.

War of the Rebellion, Series I, Vol. L, Part I.

Index

About the Author

Lt/Colonel Donald H. Shannon, US Air Force, (retired).

Military Service was in the Strategic Air Command. Was the first to be assigned to "Looking Glass," SAC's Airborne Command Post, who had served in two legs of the nuclear triad, both the manned bomber force and ICBMs.

Graduate of the Air War College, 1976.

Married to Janet; have two children and four grandchildren.

Education includes:

B.A. (Political Science), U. of Idaho, 1957

M.A. (History), Central Missouri U., 1967 while stationed at Whiteman AFB as a Minuteman Missile Combat Crew Commander. Part of his studies involved research at the Truman Library in **Independence**, where the Oregon Trail initially began.

Received Advanced Navigation & Bombardment training on his first of three assignments to Mather AFB, **Sacramento**, where the **California Trail** ended.

Was assigned for four years at Offutt AFB, NE, near **Omaha** and **Council Bluffs**, where the **Platte River Road** began.

Was stationed at **Mountain Home** AFB, ID, just north of the **South Alternate** and south of the main route of the **Oregon Trail**.

Was assigned to the **Wilder RBS** site which was on a high bluff overlooking the Snake River and the **South Alternate** route where it enters Oregon.

After retirement from the Air Force, has resided at **Caldwell**, ID, where the **Oregon Trail** crossed the Boise River at the mouth of the canyon.

Was born 1/4 mile from the **Morman Trail** in **Iowa**.

First traveled the route of the **Oregon Trail** on the **Union Pacific** RR, just after 3rd birthday.

First six years of schooling was at **Weiser** and the **Weiser Flat** where a later route of the **Oregon Trail** led to the Olds Ferry on the Snake River at Farewell Bend.

Began school in the one-room **Thousand Spring** school north of Weiser where recent research by I-OCTA member, **James McGill**, aided by past OCTA board member, **Wally Myers**, and local historians disclosed the route of the 1862 Goodale Wagon Train over an old Indian trail and, later, the old road to the Upper Country.

Snake Country Publishing

Books are Distributed and Sold by:

Caxton Press

312 Main Street

Caldwell, ID 83605–3299

1-800-657-6465

http://www.caxtonpress.com/#

View books at:

http://www.caxtonpress.com/store/snakecountry.html